Compliments of

Richard A. Gagné

Sarah Reinertsen

In a
SINGLE
BOUND

In a
SINGLE
BOUND

LOSING MY LEG, FINDING
MYSELF, AND TRAINING FOR LIFE

Sarah Reinertsen

with Alan Goldsher

Guilford, Connecticut

life

Note to Reader: The names and descriptions of some characters have been changed to protect their privacy.

GPP Life is an imprint of Globe Pequot Press.

Text designer: Sheryl P. Kober
Layout artist: Kim Burdick
Project manager: Lara Asher

Library of Congress Cataloging-in-Publication Data
Reinertsen, Sarah.
 In a single bound : losing my leg, finding myself, and training for life / Sarah Reinertsen with Alan Goldsher.
   p. cm.
 ISBN 978-0-7627-5143-3
 1. Reinertsen, Sarah. 2. Athletes—United States—Biography. 3. People with disabilities—United States—Biography. I. Goldsher, Alan, 1966- II. Title.
 GV697.R471A3 2009
 796.092—dc22
 [B]
                                                                    2009010716
Printed in the United States of America

10 9 8 7 6 5 4 3 2 1

This book is dedicated to my parents, Solveig Fuentes and Donald Reinertsen. You taught me how to be brave, how to pick myself up and carry on despite all the struggles. I know the stories in this book are emotional; we have survived tough times, and we are at a place of forgiveness. Our family has gone through an evolution and we have found peace.

Contents

❋

Introduction vii

CHAPTER 1:
Part Girl, Part Machine 1

CHAPTER 2:
Becoming a Champion 37

CHAPTER 3:
Even the Best Runners Can't Run Away 68

CHAPTER 4:
Jump at the Chance 100

CHAPTER 5:
Always Tri 124

CHAPTER 6:
I'mua 148

CHAPTER 7:
My Amazing Race 170

CHAPTER 8:
Unfinished Business 191

Epilogue 215

Sarah Reinertsen's Racing Career 223

Acknowledgments 227

About the Authors 232

Introduction

The Great Wall of China is over four thousand miles long, weighs a few dozen tons, and is, on average, about twenty-five feet high. I'm five-foot-nothing, and I weigh ninety-five pounds with my ten-pound prosthetic leg included. So the question is, given the opportunity, would I take on the Great Wall, one-on-one, even though on paper I had no shot of beating it? If I had a chance to scale one of the Seven Wonders of the World, would I go for it?

Well, for a million bucks, I'd sure give it my best shot.

❋

The two primary reasons why I went on the reality show *The Amazing Race* in 2006 were A) the possibility of unforgettable, life-altering international adventure, and B) the million dollar prize. During the nine prior seasons of *Race*, the contestants spanned the globe, hitting all seven continents, seeing places and doing things that few if any tourists would ever have a chance to experience, and that looked good to me.

As for the money, it wasn't a greed thing. My *Race* partner, Peter Harsch, and I made a pact that if we took home the million, we'd return to a couple of the countries we raced in—Vietnam, Mongolia, wherever—and do something to help out, like spearhead a plan to produce prosthetic limbs for land mine survivors. Not to sound corny or cheesy, but I live to make a difference.

But if I'm being honest, my motives weren't entirely altruistic. I mean, who couldn't find something useful to do with a million dollars? For me, a million dollars would mean buying a house, and paying off my car, and paying off my student loans. It would also allow me to do something nice for my loved ones. What with all they'd given up for me—going out of pocket to cover the costs of my prosthetic legs, my amputation, and my dozens of international races—I thought it would be cool to, at the very least, send my entire family away on an awesome vacation: my mother, stepfather, father, stepmother, brother, the whole crew. They'd made dozens of sacrifices for me, and going onto the *Race* and taking on a whole flock of difficult and/ or unpleasant tasks (for instance, eating four pounds of intestines, or riding a wild boar) to help *everybody* was the least I could do.

For the five days before the *Race* kicked off, Peter and I and our fellow racers were stashed at the Hotel Monaco in downtown Seattle. Afraid we might do some research for the race, or slip into an Internet cafe and e-mail all of our friends with specifics of our secret location, the producers did not allow us to leave the hotel. They confiscated our cell phones, and our in-room phones were shut off so we couldn't make or receive any calls whatsoever. We also weren't allowed to buy any pay-per-view movies, which left only regular old TV, *USA Today*, and our race partners to keep us occupied.

When we weren't holed up in our room, we were parked in a classroom-like conference room in the basement of the Monaco, going over the *Race* minutiae. I could tell some of the other contestants were bored, but I didn't mind the classes; for that matter, I appreciated the guidance and instruction, because much of the *Amazing Race* is a big unknown—which is the point, really. I felt better about the whole thing after they taught us the *Race's* official rules, and, more important, gave us the rundown on what to do in an emergency, and how to handle various dangerous scenarios, and the specifics of all the medications we'd been given—the Malarone for malaria, the injections for both hepatitis and Japanese encephalitis. Some found it tedious. I found it comforting.

We were not allowed to speak to other contestants until the *Race* started—after all, with free-flowing communication, some of the more ruthless (or canny, depending on how you look at it) racers might form alliances. The *Race* brain trust was so concerned about the possibility of inter-action that when we went up to our rooms after the meetings, we were escorted by a production assistant, who made certain we didn't grab one of the other racers, sneak out of the Monaco, hit the bars, and plot a winning strategy.

During the meetings, I tried to get a visual read on the competition, surreptitiously checking out the other teams and wondering, *What's this couple's story? Are they husband and wife…brother and sister? Best friends? Reformed ex-cons?* I also wanted to figure out how physically fit they all were, or, in the case of two rotund Muslim gentlemen named Bilal Abdul-Mani and Sa'eed Rudolph, how *unfit*. But even though Bilal and Sa'eed were on the chunky side, there was a chance they could have a major advantage over everybody in the room if we went to a Middle Eastern country, because one of them might speak Arabic. It dawned on me then that *The Amazing Race* wasn't only about being in good physical shape—educational background and innate intelligence were also vital. And I had my doubts about how we measured up against this competition.

By the same token, I didn't want anybody to figure out what I was about, so I wore long pants to these basement get-togethers, specifically so nobody could see my prosthetic. I blew it during the second meeting, however, when I crossed my legs, and my pants cuff rode up and showed off a bit of titanium, revealing my secret. Oops.

Back in our room, Peter and I killed time by packing, and unpacking, and repacking our two *Race* backpacks. We had to be strategic about what we took, because we'd be carrying those packs all over the world, so the less they weighed, the better. Since we didn't know where we'd be sent, we had to prepare for all climates, which meant long- and short-sleeve shirts, and long and short pants. Additionally, we had to pack rain gear, wool socks, bathing suits, and toiletries. I also had some extra silicone Dermo liners, the kind that I slide over my stump to keep my artificial leg on. I have different sizes because my stump can shrink or expand depending on the temperature or humidity, and I had to be prepared for any climate or physical challenge. Our packs got heavy quickly.

There were certain things we weren't allowed to bring: no iPods, no cell phones, no credit cards, no maps, no foreign language translation books, nothing that would give us even the slightest advantage. The only entertainment we could have on us was a single novel of our choice, but neither Peter nor I packed one, because there probably wouldn't be any place to curl up with a Stephen King book in, say, the Brazilian rain forests, or the Himalayas. (I did, however, pack my knitting, because I figured it was lighter than a book, and almost as diverting. And besides, if I finished a scarf, and it turned out nice, I might be able to sell it along the way for some extra cash.)

Even with the knitting, the liners, and the toiletries, I managed to whittle my pack down to eighteen pounds; Peter's was quite a bit heavier, around twenty-five pounds, primarily because he had to carry my extra prosthetic feet and legs. (It's worth mentioning that nobody else had to worry about carrying extra limbs, which put us a little bit behind the eight ball before the race even started.) The truth is, Peter's pack was pretty lean, in part because he didn't take nearly as many toiletries as I did, so carrying my five-pound spare knee, a couple of Allen wrenches, and a couple of screwdrivers wasn't much of a problem for him.

As for the other bag, our so-called "sequester bag," I wanted as little to do with that thing as possible.

If we were eliminated, the show's producers wouldn't allow us to go home before the end of the season, because if we showed up at our respective houses only a week, or two, or three after we left for Seattle, it would be obvious to our friends and family—and any eagle-eyed bloggers—that we didn't win the million. So we were to be sequestered at a random hotel somewhere outside of the United States, thus the "sequester bag," a suitcase filled with all the clothes and toiletries we'd need if we didn't win the *Race*.

The night before we left for the *Race*, after I finished brushing my teeth, I walked out of the bathroom and my prosthetic knee gave out. I said, "Hey Peter, I think there's something wrong here, can you check it for me?"

I took off my leg and handed it to him. He played with the hinges and vents, and noticed the metal was wet. He pointed to the liquid oozing from the knee and said, "Yup, you've blown out the hydraulic. You're leaking hydraulic fluid."

"Damn it!" I collapsed on the bed, stunned. We hadn't even started the race and my prosthetic knee was already busted. I wasn't completely screwed, but things were most definitely screwed up.

I'd blown my hydraulic knee several times—it's a natural part of the wear and tear on my mechanics. The valves on my hydraulic knee are made of rubber, and after excessive use or extreme temperatures, they can pop. A pop is normal for a knee that's been used for months and months, but the one Peter was trying to fix was only two weeks old, so apparently this one was a lemon. When my knee's hydraulic is in good shape, it moves like a nice, new, smooth screen door; when you push the door open, the momentum of the hydraulic takes over, and the door practically opens itself. But if the hydraulic dies, it acts like an old, rickety screen door, slamming shut the second you let go of it.

When it leaks, I can't control the knee. The knee controls me.

It was another pre-*Race* hiccup, but it was what it was, and I had to accept and deal with it. I'd been in dozens of competitions where I was the only disabled woman, so I was used to being at a disadvantage. But still, to already have gone through my spare knee before we even left the United States . . . well . . . DAMN IT! That's not how any athlete wants to start the biggest race of her life. And despite the fact that it was first and foremost a television show, for a million dollar prize, the *Amazing Race* really did feel like the biggest race of my life. Once I calmed down, I gave myself a pep talk: *You've been training your whole life for something like this, Sarah, and can't let a silly mechanical glitch get in the way. If you made it through the Millennium Marathon, you can make it through the* Amazing Race.

The 2000 Millennium Marathon in New Zealand was a tough race. The knee started leaking hydraulic fluid about a half hour into the race, but I managed to make it the twenty-three remaining miles, so I knew that overcoming a blown knee was possible. Sure, the marathon was only five hours, and the *Race,* if we made it to the end, would be six weeks, but I convinced myself that since I'd survived mechanical failure before, I could do it again.

I stayed positive. I moved forward.

Just like I always have.

❋

The *Amazing Race* was a different kind of race for me, because I was racing into the unknown. At that point, after triathlons, and eight marathons, I more or less knew what to expect at each course. I knew there would be somebody to meet me at the finish line, I knew there would be food and liquid, and I knew if I had any physical problems, there'd be an expert there to help me out. Now I was embarking on an adventure that could put me anywhere in the world, possibly in the middle of nowhere, possibly with nobody to give me a hand other than Peter. It was a level of anxiety and nervousness I'd never dealt with, and every moment would be captured on video, for the world to see. Heavy stuff.

So when it was time to get on the plane at Sea-Tac, Peter and I pre-boarded with the people who needed additional assistance. Truth be told, I didn't need any assistance at all, but who's going to argue with a one-legged girl? After getting a gander at our fellow racers—the majority of whom were in damn good shape—I knew if we were going to be competitive, I'd have to use any advantage I could to even out the playing field.

Our first flight: Seattle to Beijing. It was the first time the *Amazing Race* had started out in the East rather than the West. Usually the first leg was somewhere in Europe, which would've been easier for this Western girl to acclimate to. Instead, we were off to an Asian country that had completely different languages and cultures.

Time-wise, boarding early didn't give me and Peter any particular advantage—the plane wasn't leaving for Beijing without everybody on it, so it wasn't like we'd be in China before the other racers—but the quicker we got on, the better chance we'd be able to put our backpacks directly above us in the overhead. This would give us a head start getting out of the plane and hustling to our first task, a trip to the Peking Opera House, then to a restaurant that I came to think of as the Fish Eye Inn, then to an area in the middle of Beijing called the Forbidden City.

(Here's a bit of reality television insider info: Each *Race* couple had their own personal cameraman and audio person, whom we weren't allowed to be more than twenty feet away from; after all, even though it is a race, it's also a television show, and without footage and sound, for all practical purposes, the race doesn't exist. Logically enough, this is called "The Twenty Foot Rule," and even though it's the crew's responsibility to keep up with us, it was our responsibility to slow down if they fell way behind.

A hyper-competitive individual, Peter got into the habit of running ahead of the crew, and it was common for the guys hauling the heavy camera and heavier sound equipment to chase after him and yell, *"Peter, Twenty Foot Rule, Twenty Foot Rule!"* Point being, if we got on the plane early, our personal TV crew also got on the plane early and could store their camera and luggage near their seats, making a quick exit from the plane that much easier, yet another plus for us.)

As we soon learned, deplaning first wasn't a huge advantage because of what I came to think of as The Great Equalizer: customs. You might be the first team to get in the customs line, but that did not mean you would be the first to clear. Once I realized how vital it was to blow through customs, I used my disability to cut to the front of the line ("Excuse me, sir," I'd sweetly say, "but I'm having trouble standing. Would you mind if I went up ahead of you?"), which is something I've never previously considered doing. I've always prided myself on being treated like everyone else, and this made me feel dirty. But I was aware that if the other competitors were in my shoes, they'd probably do the same thing.

Right off the bat, the other contestants were pissed at us. But that wasn't my problem. I had a race to run.

No, I had a race to *win*.

Peter and I got off to a great start, thanks to a kindly Chinese businessman we met on the plane, who told us where we could exchange our American currency—the *Race* people gave us a whole $66 to work with—and gave us a map with directions to the Fish Eye Inn.

Before we got into our cab to go to the Peking Opera House, Peter wandered over to Dustin Konzelman and Kandice Pelletier—a team of two bottled blonde beauty queens whom I immediately dubbed "The Barbies"—and asked them if they'd changed their dollars into yuans. I smacked him on the arm and said, "What're you doing? Let them figure it out when they get to the restaurant and they have no money, and they're up shit creek." Peter wasn't always mindful about those sorts of things, and often didn't take the two extra seconds to think things all the way through. He wanted to be liked, and sometimes forgot that *The Amazing Race* was a game, not a popularity contest. Plus he thought The Barbies were hot.

That said, in Beijing, Peter was a phenomenal partner. I was so proud of Peter, me, the way we worked together as a team in Beijing, I only wish we could have maintained that synchronicity outside of China. Working in tandem, both on the same page, we came out like gangbusters. I think after we were the second to arrive and get seated at the Fish Eye Inn, the other racers got kind of freaked out, concerned that they'd lose to a tiny girl with one leg.

Throughout its run, *The Amazing Race* has been known to make their contestants eat some seriously gnarly food—bugs, cow lips, camel meat, you know, that sort of fare—and when we were planning our race strategy in Seattle, I told Peter, "You have to do any food challenges, because I don't have a strong stomach." He was fine with that. That is, until he found out that he had to eat a plateful of Fish Eye Inn's house special, which was, of course, fish eyes.

The waiter brought out a bowl of murky broth with four fish heads floating on the surface, and four heads meant eight eyeballs, all of which Peter had to force down his gullet. The fish soup smelled disgusting—it was like being at your local fish market at the end of the day—and the heads looked frightening. But slowly, very slowly, one at a time, with the *Race* officials watching every lift of his chopsticks, Peter shoved down those gross white, slimy, slippery balls. Aside from telling him to swallow the eyes as if they were pills, I wasn't much help. (As a matter of fact, my weak stomach was screwing Peter up; as he chewed on eye number five, he told me, "You have to stop gagging, because you're making me gag.") When he polished off the final fish eye, we hopped a cab and it was off to the Forbidden City.

The taxi dropped us—as well as two other teams—about eight hundred meters away from where we needed to be, so it turned into a foot race. I'd practiced running with a backpack, so I found my rhythm, set a nice pace, and tried to keep up with Peter. We zipped by both teams, but after about a hundred meters, I stumbled; and we still had a small lead, ahead I could see the lights from the *Race* finish area off in the distance, and I couldn't stop running.

Good thing I didn't, because we were the first team to arrive. It didn't win us any prizes, but I was proud (and somewhat vindicated) to have had such a solid start. As we waited for the other teams, I caught my breath and noticed that my spare knee was screwed up big-time. More leaky hydraulic fluid. Unbelievable. One day, two blown prosthetic knees. But I was damned if I was going to give up.

The next morning, after a few hours of fitful sleep, we were given our next big task: Navigate on a motorbike through the streets of Beijing, build a sidewalk near a local market, then make our way to scale the Great Wall of China.

In this instance, I wasn't sure as to the exact definition of "scale"—you can't take anything at face value on the show, because to keep us on our toes, they make sure all their task clues are tricky and/or nebulous. In the real world, scaling means, you know, *scaling,* but I guessed that in *The Amazing Race* world, scaling meant climbing a whole bunch of stairs to get to the top of the Wall. Besides, I knew there was no way the Chinese government would let us crawl up the side of the thing.

I was wrong. Scaling meant scaling.

Even though I was kind of nervous about how it was going to play out, I was still amped about seeing one of the Seven Wonders of the World. The Beijing cabbies, however, weren't amped to take us to the Wall, because the chances of them getting a fare back into the city were slim at best. So we gave a driver the entire contents of our wallets—we only had about $30 of our $66 left, a decent fare for a ride of that distance—because we were well aware that if we didn't make it to the Wall, our *Race* would be over before it even started.

Knots formed in my stomach, and the nasty breakfast wasn't to blame; this was out-and-out fear. Save for a few sessions on the climbing wall at Chelsea Piers in New York City, I'd never done any rock climbing, so I was wandering into the great physical unknown. Another issue: The two-legged competitors would definitely have an easier time scaling. Peter tried to hype me up, saying "You're a world class athlete, Sarah. You're going to be fine. You've done the Ironman World Championships, the toughest triathlon in the world, you know how to be tough and I know you'll scale this thing, no problem." I was glad he thought so.

There were two entrances to the area of the Great Wall where we'd been told to meet; one was at ground level, and one wasn't. We were on the lower level, but it seemed easy enough to get up to the next level, where the cameras were all set up. We ran up one set of stairs, and came to a dead end. We ran down the stairs, back to another set of stairs and hit another dead end. We peered at the tippy-top of the Wall; there was a camera crew, and a bunch of ropes dangling down the side. We realized that's where we had to get to, but in the maze of stairs and landings, we couldn't figure out how to get there. After almost half an hour of clueless wandering, we finally found the stairwells that took us to the correct side of the Wall.

After all the confusion, I figured the hard part was over. Unfortunately, I figured wrong.

I'm under a microscope when I'm at a triathlon—there aren't too many short, blonde above-the-knee amputees at your typical race, so I tend to stand out—but since I'm comfortable in the water, or on a bike, or on the road, it never bothers me when another triathlete or a race watcher gives me an in-depth once-over, because I know I look like I know what I'm doing. Climbing the Wall in front of a battalion of television cameras was a whole other story. The entire television viewing world was going to see me looking, well, who knew *how* I was going to look? Clumsy? Silly? Freaked out? Only time would tell.

As I put on my harness, I stared up into the bright morning sky. From my position, the Wall looked about the same height as my old Brooklyn apartment. The height was bad, but the fact that it was a straight shot without any big ridges or lips in the concrete to grab onto was worse. It was nothing like what I'd climbed during my training sessions at Chelsea Piers.

The rope had loops tied along the length of it that were, in effect, my stairs. The way that the loops were tied made it unbelievably difficult for somebody with one leg; it was virtually impossible for me to plant my prosthetic. I had no leverage. It had to be all arms. I'd have to hold my body in midair, find the next loop, and pull myself up. And then again. And then again. And then again. My upper body was in good shape—I'd been lifting weights for over ten years at that point—but I hadn't trained for this. For that matter, *nobody* had, because *nobody* scales the Great Wall.

After only three loops, my arms were on fire, and there were about twenty-five more loops to go. I glared at the top of the wall and thought, *Holy shit . . . what did I sign up for here . . . I'm in over my head . . . I don't know if I can do this . . . but this is what you asked for, Sarah . . . you wanted to do* The Amazing Race, *so here you are.* I'd always considered myself a badass, but I had a mini meltdown: tears, high-pitched whining, just like a panicked school kid. (After this episode of *Race* aired, my friends started calling me Sarah Whine-ertsen. Nice friends, right?) I dangled there for a moment, letting the harness hold my weight as I gently swung and rested my arms for a minute, then came up with a mantra: *You have the strength to do this . . . show them that you're tougher than the rest.* It worked. Loop by loop by loop, I inched my way up. That became my m.o. for the rest of the season: Freak out for a moment, then give myself a pep talk, then muster up the strength to take on whatever challenge was in front of me.

(By the way, I should note that our season was a helluva lot harder than any other season to that point. They stepped it up, but they had to—this was their thenth year on air, and they couldn't let the show get stale. In the early *Race* days, many of the tasks were brainless: For instance, a contestant was assigned to find some plastic gnomes in the middle of a field. Halfway up the side of the wall, I wondered why those season three chumps got to search for lawn ornaments, while we had to climb up a vertical wall.)

Thirty minutes later, sweaty, teary, and every muscle screaming, I was at the top of the wall. One of the cameramen pulled me aside and said, "I've shot every season of this show, and that was one of the most incredible moments we've ever had. That's something I'll never forget."

That made two of us.

When Peter got to the top, *Race* host Phil Keoghan told us that we were one of the top three teams, but as amped as I was that we'd finished ahead of some serious competition, I wasn't satisfied. I thought, *Man, if I had two legs, we'd be in the lead*—but then again, if I had two legs, I probably wouldn't have been on the show in the first place.

Winning the theoretical bronze medal in the first leg of the *Race* was unbelievably satisfying, especially since it wasn't a cakewalk task like collecting lawn ornaments. Peter and I showed the world that we were formidable competitors, even if there were only three good legs between the two of us.

Later that night, I stared at the Wall from our hotel room, thinking, *We're in China. We're at the Great Wall. People come to this country from all over the world to see this place. And how many of them get to scale it? None. They climb the stairs, but I climbed the side. This is the only manmade landmark you can see from outer space, and I got to climb it.* I reveled in the knowledge that I'd scaled this monument, and believed that since I handled that hurdle, I could conquer even greater heights. If the Great Wall of China wasn't big enough to stop me, nothing would. If one little person could scale the side of one of Earth's greatest landmarks, one little person could take on the world.

CHAPTER 1

PART GIRL, PART MACHINE

Things were tense in the delivery room.

First off, it was a breech birth, and breech births are scary as hell for everybody. The tension grew exponentially when the nurse said, "Doctor, can you please come and look at this?"

"What's wrong?"

The nurse gestured at my legs. My left leg was shorter than my right leg.

The doctor didn't freak out. He told my mother, "Don't worry. It's possible that the leg was pushed up during the delivery, and will fall back into place."

Mom and Dad were alarmed, of course, but all they wanted to do was hold their new baby girl, so they didn't freak out, either. They even stayed cool the following day when the orthopedist gave them my diagnosis: proximal femoral focal deficiency.

Proximal femoral focal deficiency. When a birth defect has a big, scary name, it sometimes makes it sound more severe than it really is. That wasn't the case here. Proximal femoral focal deficiency—or, in layman's terms, a shortened leg bone that'll never grow—is as bad as it sounds.

※

My mother Solveig and my father Don were just like any other new parents: They expected their first child to have ten perfect fingers, and ten perfect toes, and two perfect arms, and two perfect legs. What is supposed to be the most exciting moment for a new parent didn't feel like a dream come true, but rather a kind of nightmare. I've always imagined my parents sitting in their living room right after bringing me home from the hospital, staring at each other, elated and joyful that they'd had a mostly healthy daughter, but petrified about the child's major medical issue, whispering some variation of, *What the hell are we going to do now?*

And that was more than a fair question, because at that point, in the less-enlightened mid-1970s, there wasn't any kind of support network for parents of proximal femoral focal deficiency babies near our house on Long Island, New York. Mom and Dad didn't know anybody who had a disabled child. They didn't have the Internet or useful books to research their newborn's birth defect. They didn't know where to go, or whom to talk to. They had to make it up as they went along.

I was a tiny baby—we're talking only five pounds at birth—and for most of my first year, my mismatched legs weren't much of a hindrance, so I was able to crawl around our house without any kind of brace. I was able to eventually stand, but when I started to walk at eleven months, balance and my wobbly gait became a problem, so it was off to the Eschen Prosthetic and Orthotic Lab.

Eschen, where I received the first of many leg braces, was located a good hour away, in a not-so-good section of Spanish Harlem. Coming from suburban Long Island in our tan 1980 Volkswagen Rabbit, we stood out like four lily-white sore thumbs. We'd park the car, and *always* make sure the doors were locked.

The neighborhood was a foreign country. There was a bodega across the street from the clinic, and one day, Dad ran over to get a snack, and returned with what he thought was a bag of potato chips, but, in reality, were fried pork rinds. He took one bite, grimaced, looked at the bag, and told my mother, "I don't think they sell chips over there, you know what I mean?"

I had no idea what he meant, so I asked, "If they don't sell chips, does that mean they just sell chocolate? Or candy? Or soda?" Dad just shook his head and chuckled.

Eschen's front door was thick metal, covered in graffiti, and all patients had to be buzzed into the building—in that neighborhood, you couldn't be too cautious. The secretaries and assistants all had long nails, and big hair, and I loved listening to them speaking in their rapid-fire Spanish, with their Nuyorican accents. (In fourth grade, I took after-school Spanish lessons, and right after the first class, the teacher asked Mom, "Do you guys have a nanny who speaks Spanish? Sarah's accent is *impeccable*.") I felt more connected to the big-haired girls in the front than I did to the white-coated guys in the back.

The Eschen prosthetists were all men—one of whom I remember reeked of cigarettes. Some of them were tall and skinny, and some had big bellies, but all of them were scary, what with their poking, and prodding, and writing down who-knows-what-kind of figures, and nodding knowingly but silently.

My first prosthetic was a flesh-colored hard plastic/polymer frame. When I'd slide my little leg inside, my real toes pointed down, and the brace evened out the height of my legs. The bottom of the brace had an infant-sized foot made of wood, wrapped with smooth, flesh-toned leather. In order to make my brace, the doctors had to get measurements from the bottom of my foot to the very top of my thigh, which meant their tape measures ended up right near my *stuff.* Mom dressed me up to go to the appointments—she *always* made it a point to put me in cute clothes, the leg issues notwithstanding—and I'd be sitting there in my underwear, in front of all these guys, usually close to tears, my nice little girly-girl outfit forgotten. The doctors and my parents tried to make the process more comfortable for me, but eventually, after years of being poked and prodded, I went into immediate hysterics at the sight of *anyone* in a white coat. As soon as the doctor walked into the room, I'd hold down my skirt and scream, "NoNoNoNoNo! Get away from me!"

Mom held my hand to calm me down and told me that it would be okay, but there's only so much you can do to relax a three-year-old. When all else failed they bribed me with the promise of ice cream. Unfortunately, I almost always fell asleep in the car on the way home from sheer exhaustion from the visit, and would completely forget about the promised treat.

So all in all, the whole thing sucked.

❄

Mom's family immigrated to the United States from Norway in 1955 and immediately settled in the Norwegian-centric Bay Ridge section of Brooklyn. (It's now a predominantly Korean area, but there are two remnants of the old Norwegian days: the legendary Leske's Bakery, and the Atlantic Scandinavian Diner, which, in a true sign of the times, now shares the restaurant with a Korean family and serves many Asian dishes.) Dad and his family, who were also from Norway, were already in Bay Ridge. It was all but fated that Solveig Sandvik and Don Reinertsen would hook up.

They met at Trinity Lutheran Church in Brooklyn, where they sang in the summer youth choir. Back then, Trinity had services delivered in Norwegian, which my parents' families loved, because hearing a group of people speak in their native tongue helped give them a sense of community. The church was also a place for them to connect with other Norwegians, which was important to Mom's family, as they were pretty strict about whom she socialized with. And it wasn't just Mom's parents who were concerned with her friends; her brother Helge—and I should note that Helge with an "E" is a man's name in Norway—took it upon himself to shoo away potentially unacceptable suitors from Solveig. His shooing usually went along the lines of, "Don't talk to my sister. You're Italian." Being Norwegian, and a churchgoer to boot, Dad received a thumbs-up. (Dad was actually the choir director, and my mom was in the choir. Truth be told, my mom had a beautiful voice, and I'm sure he partly fell in love with her because she is such a beautiful singer.)

Dad was a hard worker. He taught music at the local high school, *plus* he gave private piano lessons at our house, *plus* he was our church's organist and choir director. Music teachers don't make much money, and when you have a child with an expensive disability, you have to do what you have to do. Mom was a part-time choreographer in the Commack and Northport school districts, and she loved it so much that she ended up choreographing some local community theater shows, and teaching private dance, all of which she did at night, in order to be with me and my younger brother Peter during the day.

My parents' work ethic was stellar, which was fortunate because we needed all the financial help we could get, primarily to pay for the care and feeding of my leg. Our insurance plan was horrible; my first leg brace—which cost about $900—was covered in full . . . and that was it. There were always insane out-of-pocket expenses; with each new prosthetic, Mom and Dad submitted claims over and over, some of which were covered, and some of which weren't. The most the insurance companies ever paid was 80 percent; the remaining 20 percent was so costly that they couldn't always pay the balance in full and were forced to take out loans. They became rabid advocates and fought the big companies hard, and were sometimes lucky to have some of our church's parishioners fighting and fundraising alongside them. We needed all the help we could get.

❀

We lived about half a mile from the Bay Hills beach, and during the summer, we were there almost every day. My family and their friends made it a point to keep me insulated in a circle of kind, supportive people, so I had no problem taking off my brace and hopping across the sand.

When I turned four, however, I became acutely aware that everybody else looked different in a bathing suit than I did. That didn't keep me from my appointed rounds, but once in a while, I felt like a freak. Especially when someone new was at the beach, they'd be staring at me as if I were a rare animal who'd escaped from the Long Island Zoo. Fortunately, most of the beachgoers who saw me hopping from our towel to the ocean thought, *Oh, that's just Sarah,* so most of the time, it was okay.

On a day-to-day basis, I was basically a pretty happy kid, but sometimes I'd ask Mom, "Why do I have to have this leg? I *hate* it."

She'd tell me, "You can't do anything about it. It's not something that can be fixed with cough syrup. Go out and play, and have fun, and don't worry about it." She also compared my leg to my Dad's glasses. "Your father needs his glasses to see, just like you need your brace to walk. It's no big deal."

I know other female amputees whose parents put them in long dresses in order to hide the handicap, almost instilling in them shame about their missing leg. That was most definitely not how Solveig did things. Mom always treated me like any other kid. It was never, *Let's get Sarah some watercolors, and have her sit inside and paint all day.* She'd take me outside and I played with all the other kids, swung on the swing set, climbed the jungle gym, played duck-duck-goose, and was the best hopscotch player in the neighborhood. And when I fell, Mom taught me to pick myself up, which sometimes led to some dirty looks from the other parents. But she knew I'd eventually have to take care of myself, so why not get me started early? Never once did I question it.

A couple months after I turned seven, we went on our semi-annual visit to the New York University hospital for my orthopedic check-up. It was time to talk about the options for "fixing my leg." The leg wouldn't literally be fixed—there wasn't a cure for proximal femoral focal deficiency—but my parents and doctors wanted to figure out a way for me to live as comfortable a life as possible.

The concept of amputation had been thrown around, which I naturally didn't like to hear about. But there was a silver lining: If I lost my leg, I'd lose my brace, and that would be a good thing because that damn thing wasn't even close to comfortable.

It had a hard frame, a leg-length boot that didn't breathe, and had zero give. Also, it was a pain to put on; the process involved wearing really long wool or cotton socks, then sliding my leg into the prosthetic with my toes pointing down, then strapping Velcro strips across the leg and around my waist. It was ugly, uncomfortable, and smelly, and my stump would often get sweaty and chafed if I was outside all day playing. Gross.

I also wasn't thrilled about how bad the leg looked, especially the way my feet never matched. Yes, the leg was part of my body, but on a certain level, I found it hideous. It felt freakish that I had this weird little leg with the foot dangling in midair, and I spent a lot of time staring at my one good leg, and willing the little leg to just grow and catch up. It was weird and sort of ugly, but I couldn't entirely hate it, because it was part of me. It was a conundrum: Embrace the leg as my own, or disown it because it was ugly.

I tried to put a positive spin on it, telling myself that it was okay to be different, that I was a rare bird, unique and unlike anyone else I knew. I sincerely believed that yes, this thing made me special, so why should I hate that? Isn't it good to be special? I think many fully able people feel that way about certain parts of their body, too. Somebody might be just as embarrassed by her nose, or her hips, or her ears. We all want to change something on our bodies, and in my case, it happened to be my leg.

My parents involved me in the decision and took me to all the meetings at New York University Hospital with my specialist Dr. Selene Jaramillo. Even though Dr. Jaramillo was a caring, compassionate woman, I often dreaded seeing her, because she was a teaching professor, which meant that at many of my exams, she'd come into the room with ten students in tow, and I'd be sitting there in my underwear, and she'd draw on my leg with a red ballpoint pen as if it were a blackboard, or maybe a medical chart. I felt more like an object than a human being.

My leg had never hurt me, so I asked Dr. Jaramillo, "Why do we even need to fix this? It isn't really broken. It's the only left leg I have, so why are you going to take it away from me?"

Dr. Jaramillo patiently explained: "You have three options, Sarah. We could surgically give you an internal prosthetic, and that will lengthen your legs to the same height, but it would also mean that you'll have to have surgeries every time you grow. The second choice is to have part of your left leg amputated so that you could wear a better prosthetic leg, and this procedure would require only two surgeries. If we go that route, you'll have a clean stump so we can get you a better leg, one with a knee that bends in the same place as everyone else's, instead of a stiff leg that doesn't bend at all. Or we can do nothing at all and leave the leg exactly as it is."

It took a while, but I eventually began to understand the basics of the situation—my left leg wasn't like my right leg, and it would get worse as I got older, and it would be good for me down the line for the left leg to be removed—but the science went right over my head. I didn't know what tissue was, or what a bone was, or why I had to have multiple surgeries. Even though I didn't understand the complexities, I chose amputation.

After we scheduled the appointment for the surgery, my parents prepared me as best they could. They bought me children's books about hospitals, and we visited the NYU children's ward and the rehab wing so I would have a clear understanding of where I would have to live for a couple months. They tried to comfort me, and I tried to be brave, but I was scared.

I was so wrapped up in my own situation that I didn't even realize the toll it was taking on my parents. Raising two children while holding down a job (or two, or three) is hard enough, even without having to schlep in and out of Spanish Harlem on a regular basis. But Mom was the CEO of the family, and an excellent one at that, so she managed to keep it together.

And just like that, it was surgery time. At the first operation, they fused my knee—which, at that point, was right near the middle of my thigh—then put my little leg in a cast, with my left toes sticking out of the bottom, so the bones could set. Dr. Jaramillo explained that by doing the knee fusion, we could monitor the toes and the leg for infection. When the bones healed, it was time for surgery number two, the actual amputation. They removed the foot, then wrapped the heel pad around the base of the stump, so that my heel was the bottom of my stump, and was able to bear weight since the heel is a weight-bearing bone.

After the amputation, for the first time during this whole mess, I was hurting, big-time. It felt like somebody was repeatedly stabbing my leg with a knife. On a scale of one to ten, the pain was about a twelve, far worse than anything I've experienced before or since. The nights were the worst, when the pain seemed most intense and I couldn't sleep. I constantly begged for pain medications, which, thanks to some long and scary needles, were painful in and of themselves, but when the drugs kicked in, for a brief while, there'd be a whole lot of *ahhhhhhhhh*. And finally I could sleep and rest for just a bit until the painkillers wore off.

And then there was the phantom pain where my left toes used to be. (My theory about phantom pain—which feels like real pain, by the way—is that it's the body's way of mourning the loss of a limb, the kind of mourning you feel after a loved one dies. But pain isn't the only phantom-like aspect of amputation—to this day, I still feel like I can wiggle my left toes.) I used to refer to phantom pain as Chinese torture . . . which I now know is a racist and awful thing to say, but I *was* only seven.

They kept me at NYU for two months to rest and recover, and I was sent to the Rusk Rehab Institute for Physical Therapy for another month. Mom stayed with me the whole time. For those three months, she slept in one of those uncomfortable reclining hospital visitor chairs, but I'm sure she got more rest being next to my bed than she would have if she were at home, forty miles away, not knowing what was going on with her one-legged daughter.

At NYU, we were shuffled through several hospital rooms, one of which I shared with an eight-year-old who had a brain tumor. I looked at my bandaged, immovable stump, then stared at the shunt on that poor girl's head, and thought, *At least that's not me.* Sometimes even seven-year-old amputees can manage some perspective.

I went home in a wheelchair, which meant Dad had to retrofit the house so I'd be able to both get into the front door and move around the first floor. Dad was a pretty handy guy, so he happily got the lumber and built it all himself; unfortunately he wasn't able to build a ramp up to the second floor where my bedroom was, so I had to sleep on the sofa in the living room. I was bedridden for three months—or couch-ridden, I suppose—but my friends and family's friends did what they could to keep up my spirits. The church youth group all pitched in and bought me an Atari video game console, as well as an Indiana Jones game, Pac-Man, and Space Invaders, all of which Peter and

I played constantly. The neighborhood kids also came by, and my teachers brought over homework, and all my classmates wrote me letters—they were probably ordered to do so, but it was still nice to get them. My life was all about sitting around and healing, but I got antsy quick. It takes time to mend, which is hard for a kid to understand.

Not long after I returned home, we had some incredible snowstorms that closed down our schools for an entire week. All the kids from the block were on the streets building forts, and riding their sleds, and having snowball fights, and it sucked sitting by the window and watching them having fun without me. I was missing out on the most awesome snowfall of the century, so awesome that it felt like a national holiday. Life seemed even more cruel and unfair as I watched the kids run past with their bright winter coats through our white snow-covered lawn.

My parents recognized how bummed out I was, so Dad shoveled out the sidewalk and the driveway, and Mom bundled me up, and I was wheeled out to the end of the driveway. All I could do was watch, but at least I had a better view. Everybody treated me wonderfully, but I was still robbed of the coolest winter ever.

By the end of March, the pins were removed, and when they took off the bandages, I couldn't even recognize my skin as my own. My new stump was all yellow from the Betadine, and covered with crusty blood. Logically I knew it was my body, but it didn't look right; it was scary and ugly and I was horrified. All I could say was, "Is that really my leg? Is that *really* my leg? Is that really *my* leg?" When the pins were removed, my stump went off like a gusher. There was blood everywhere, and I felt like I didn't even own that part of my body anymore. Once the bleeding stopped, I stared at the stump and thought, *This is gross. Plus it stinks.* But I could finally get off of Couch Island, and very carefully crutch my way up the stairs and into my bedroom and sleep in my own bed for the first time in forever.

And then, before I could even get a tiny bit acclimated to a one-legged life, it was back to Eschen again. And again. And again.

The trips to Harlem now meant doing up a mold for the prosthetic leg. I would put on a body stocking and they would wrap my stump with plaster of Paris tape. After the mold was dry, the prosthetist would remove it with a buzz saw, and that always freaked me out. It didn't hurt, but it was still scary, and I'd scream and grab my mother as the blade bore down on me, and its noise zapped through my head.

My first prosthetic was made from a shiny, flesh-toned wood/plastic compound, and had hinges at the knee and a hollow bottom. It was like a Barbie doll leg, except harder, a free-swinging hunk with a rubber foot. There were no hydraulics, it was totally unstable, and it made an annoying snapping noise with every step. (My family made up raps about the damn thing, for instance, "Sarah's leg is so loud, you can always find her in a crowd." They also liked to tell me that I could never be a burglar, because everybody would hear me coming.) It was an antiquated piece of equipment, but we didn't bother looking for another type of prosthetic, because we were dealing with NYU, one of the great medical centers in New York, and if NYU said Eschen was the place, then Eschen was the place. We were all such novices that we didn't know there were other options out there.

As was the case with the rest of my body, my right leg was completely healthy, and grew at a proportionate rate, which meant that whenever I had a growth spurt, we had to schlep out to Eschen and get a new leg that fit me. To give you some perspective on that, a typical parent has to buy their growing kid new shoes about four times a year; that's how often I needed a new prosthetic. Between fifth grade and seventh grade, I was at Eschen almost once a month, again getting poked and prodded by those good ol' boys in their good ol' white coats.

Getting the Barbie legs was a relatively painless process, so by the time I was nine, I accepted the fact that this was just part of my life. Like my parents' car, I would have to get an "oil and lube" on my artificial leg, and that would be the deal for the rest of my life, because my left leg was gone for good.

❊

All the kids in the neighborhood rode bikes, and I wanted in. My parents thought it would be doable—biking would certainly be easier and probably safer than running—so for my ninth birthday, they bought me a powder blue Schwinn with a banana seat, which I immediately covered with flower stickers. (It should be noted that flower stickers were the height of coolness.) Mom and Dad had black plastic toe straps installed onto the pedals to keep my foot secure, but sometimes the Barbie leg slipped out of the strap, and it was nearly impossible to get it back in while the bike was moving. We considered taping my foot to the pedal, but then I'd always be locked onto the bike, which would've been a tad problematic if I fell.

My dad was in charge of the riding lessons; first he put the training wheels on, and we just tried getting my balance in the driveway. Eventually we went out on the road, and Dad would hold the back of the seat while I pedaled to make sure I was steady enough. Eventually, I got comfortable riding in a nearby parking lot and on flat roads, but I never totally mastered hills.

Six weeks later—when the training wheels finally came off, and I more or less had my bearings—I went on my first ride with Peter and his friends. It was one loop in our neighborhood, down Soundview Drive to the beach, then down Huntington Bay Road and back up to our house. It was so exciting to be out on the road with the other kids, after watching them do their thing for years.

The ride started out okay. I was fine going downhill, but then we hit a false flat—that's when the road appears level to the naked eye, but there's actually a slight incline—and I was done. I couldn't keep up with them, even on a tiny hill that didn't really look like a hill, and I thought, *God, I suck.* At the bottom of the hill, I got off the bike, pushed it home, and stuck it into the back of our garage. It was mortifying that my little brother and his friends, who were all three years younger than me, were tearing down the street, and I couldn't keep up with them on what, for all practical purposes, was a flat road.

I didn't touch a bicycle for another seventeen years.

Dad had a temper, and he didn't always know how to keep it in check. He'd been gentle with Peter and me when we were infants, but by the time I was eight and Peter was five—the point at which he believed we were old enough to understand and take direction—his incessant rage became a serious problem. Sure, parents have the right to get angry and upset with their children, but they have to channel their anger in a productive, positive manner, something that Dad was unable to do. When he'd get pushed to the edge—or at least when he *felt* like he was being pushed—he'd become abusive. Sometimes it was physical. Sometimes it was verbal. And sometimes it was both.

There never seemed to be a direct correlation between the severity of our supposed misbehavior and the reprimand. We were often harshly punished for a seemingly innocuous transgression, like if we didn't pick up after ourselves, we might get pulled up the stairs by our hair. Or if we didn't take out the garbage, we might get our head shoved and held against the wall. Or if we got into a typical sibling fight during a long car ride, we might get punched in the chest with a closed fist.

Or if I didn't do the dishes while he was teaching a private piano lesson in the living room, he'd threaten to hide my prosthetic leg. Or if I mouthed off, he'd threaten to not take me to Eschen for my new leg. He never actually followed through on either of those, but I believed that he would.

The worst of it—the thing that ultimately messed up our heads the most—was that thanks to Dad's incessant putdowns, Peter and I never felt like we did anything right. Our grades were never high enough, and we were never good enough musicians, and we screwed up everything.

Yes, Dad worked long days, and yes, our money was tight, and he was undoubtedly stressed all the time, but that didn't give him the right to take his frustrations out on us. You don't tell your daughter you're going to take away the prosthetic leg that gives her mobility, or threaten to not take her to the next doctor's appointment. You have to be bigger and better than that. You have to rise above.

Sunday mornings were particularly dicey. Church started at 9:00, and we had to be there by 8:30 so Dad could warm up with the choir. There was almost always a lot of rushing around—sometimes Mom would have to come and wake me up a couple times, or sometimes Peter couldn't find a clean pair of slacks—and the atmosphere in our house was *intense,* so it wouldn't take much for Dad to lose his patience. He'd yell and scream at me, or start a blowout fight with my mother, or pick up Peter, carry him upstairs, and hurl him onto his bed. (My brother suffered more of Dad's physical abuse because A) he was a guy, and B) he wasn't disabled.)

After yet another World War III blowout at the house, we'd show up at church, all dolled up in our nice clothes, looking like the perfect, well-adjusted, blonde-haired, blue-eyed, completely all-American family. It was bizarre going from a hate- and rage-filled morning to singing hymns about peace being with us.

I never told anybody what was going on with my father: no friends, no family, no *nobody.* There was something a little satisfying in the fact that I was able to make everything seem okay to the outside world, that I could fool everybody into thinking that I came from the perfect family. Peter never said a word either. We were never coached to keep it under wraps, but secrecy was so embedded in our family system, we never even considered spilling the beans.

I always felt Dad wanted to stop himself from hurting us, but his rage was so intense that he simply couldn't. What made it even worse was that his boiling point was different every day. We never knew if something as innocuous as, say, forgetting to brush our teeth would lead to a garden variety tongue-lashing, or off-the-charts insanity. That said, he never seriously marked us; there were a couple bruises here and there, but he never broke any bones, or made us bleed.

Truth be told, his most powerful, most effective weapon was his words.

When I was in the fifth grade, Dad and I had a big blow-out about some trivial, forgettable matter, and it became heated, with more screaming than usual. I looked at the clock, and saw that if I didn't get the hell out of the house, I'd miss the bus, or go nuts, or possibly both. So I threw on my jacket, ran to the front door, spun around and said, "Dad, just fuck off, okay," and then I rushed out of the house and slammed the door behind me before he could say another word. Cursing at him was both scary and liberating. I must've freaked Dad out, because there wasn't ever any specific retribution.

One of the big tenets of Christianity is to always forgive, a tenet so ingrained in me that I always looked for the love inside my father. When he apologized for hurting me, I always forgave him, but I was also always wary, because I never knew the next time he'd boil over. The concepts of "honor thy father" and "honor thy child" were alive and well in our church, but not in the Reinertsen living room.

※

Just before he turned forty, Dad went to his doctor for his yearly physical and was told he had both high cholesterol and high blood pressure. (The cholesterol was genetic. The blood pressure was part genetic, and part self-inflicted.) The doctor said, "If you want to live to be around for your kids, you're going to need to start exercising." Having lost his own father in his teens, this hit Dad in the gut, so he started running. The timing was perfect, as this was near the end of the running boom of the early 1970s, a time when casual runners were finally being taken seriously; nobody thought it was crazy to see a semi-out-of-shape, shirtless thirtysomething jogging down the street.

Dad began running regularly in 5K and 10K races, and his favorite was the Harry Chapin Memorial Run Against Hunger. Every year, he'd drag me and Peter along, and make us do the kids' races, which I hated, because I always finished dead last. The Barbie leg wasn't made for competitive running, but even if it was, I didn't know how to move quickly in a prosthetic leg. All I learned at the physical therapy hospital was how to walk up and down the hall.

When I was eleven, Dad entered a 10K out in Plainview, specifically because he'd heard through the grapevine that there was going to be a female amputee at the race. "She's a runner," he told me, "and it might be cool for you to come with me and hang out with her."

I was about to start sixth grade and was entering a phase when I didn't want to do anything that my parents asked me to do, no matter how cool it might've been, so I said, "Daaaaad, why do I have to get up early on a Saturday? I don't want to go to your stupid race. And why do I have to talk to this person. Who is she, God?" (Ironically, this woman soon became somewhat of a deity to me.) Simply put, I was being a whiny preteen.

But I went to the race, and, a few minutes after I got settled, this woman blows by us, running on an artificial leg. She was smooth, and graceful, and running beautifully, not to mention that she was *fast*, even faster than my father.

After the race, I was introduced to Paddy Rossbach.

Paddy was a petite fortysomething with a sharp English accent and was extremely cool. She told me that she'd lost her leg at six, when she was run over by a truck, and she was amputated below the knee. I pointed to her uncovered prosthetic, a prosthetic where you could clearly see the futuristic-looking black carbon fiber pylon, and said, "It's amazing you can run on that thing."

She said, "Well, you can learn to run, too. I've done nine marathons."

I stared at her leg and said, "Whoa. You've run marathons on that thing? My *Dad* hasn't even run a marathon." The marathon was special to us Reinertsens, because nine-time New York Marathon winner Grete Waitz was from Norway. Civic pride.

"You can do it too, if you want." She handed me a business card. "Have your parents call me."

Paddy headed up a program out of Sloan-Kettering Hospital in Manhattan called ASPIRE (Adolescent Sarcoma Patients Intense Rehabilitation with Exercise—a great group with a convoluted acronym). She helped rehab cancer patients who'd lost limbs from cancer, but she eventually expanded the program to work with any and all amputees. The program's primary focus: *exercise*.

Paddy did a study that proved amputees used twice the energy and 40 percent more oxygen than a person with two legs, so cardiovascularly, we're not as efficient. We need to work a whole lot harder than everybody else to keep up—after all, we're lugging along our prosthetic, a piece of dead weight that's not connected to our brain. Paddy's theory was that the more we exercise, the more we rehabilitate, and the more we rehabilitate, the more efficient we'll be. That sounds simple, but, well, it's not, because many amputees don't know how to either run or ride bikes.

Paddy opened up the world for me. She became my hero, my role model, on par with Michael Jordan. She was athletic, smart, beautiful, and not only could she run marathons, she had a husband, and an important job at the hospital. In meeting her, I finally saw that, yes, you can have a normal life as an amputee. She altered my perception of what I could and couldn't do, so when she introduced me to a Long Island–based physical therapist who she said could teach me how to run, I was ready.

Enter David Balsley.

✳

David Balsley was crazy.

When I first met David—a physical therapist by day, and a nutty runner guy by night—he was training for a race called The Western States. The Western States is run outside of Sacramento, California, and it's one hundred miles run on trails, at high altitude, one shot, no resting. David finished it in seventeen hours. And he'd run it again as soon as he had the opportunity. You see what I mean by crazy?

He and Paddy showed me that human beings can do so much more than what's conventionally believed. You've got Paddy running marathons on one leg, and you've got David running for almost a full day on two legs. I couldn't wrap my head around it.

In addition to his work on the Island, David had a private practice in Manhattan . . . plus he had three children . . . plus he was always preparing for some insane race or another. In order to fit everything in, he'd wake up at 3:00 a.m., strap on his backpack, and run from his home on Long Island to his office in the city, because it was the only chance for him to squeeze in his forty-mile training run. (He once got pulled over by a policeman while he was running on the shoulder of the Long Island Expressway. The officer told him it was illegal to jog on the L.I.E., so David asked the cop, "How else am I supposed to get into the city?" The cop's answer was to give him a ticket.)

At our first session, David stuck me on a treadmill, cranked up the speed, said, "If the treadmill's too fast, you got to jump off yourself," and then he walked away. He wasn't using kid gloves with the disabled girl; he was tough, and he was teaching me how to be tough, and there'd be no complaining or short cuts.

At first, balancing on the prosthetic leg was a pain in the ass, so I did drill after drill after drill until I felt at least somewhat comfortable. We did strengthening exercises to work my stump, my left hip, and my left back especially so I could quickly and efficiently fling the prosthetic leg out in front of me. All my running exercises were done inside on the treadmill, or outside in the parking lot, and I fell *a lot*. I would run for a few steps, then land on the knee wrong, or not kick my leg out fast enough, and *crash, boom,* a face-plant. Scrapes and strawberries notwithstanding, I always got up. Even on my worst days, Dave never let me quit; I'd work until I got at least a few good strides in. He had a great way of knowing when to push me, and when to back off a bit, but never really cut me much slack, and that's exactly what you need from a coach. It took me about four months to do a consistent "leg-over-leg" stride, and it was more than worth the effort.

Eventually he took me out to a track where I could practice running on a flat surface. Dave worked me hard, and I loved it! I was so used to being the kid who was pitied in gym class, the one that the gym teacher didn't really expect much from, but to Dave, I wasn't an amputee, I was just another client whom he wanted to run to death. We worked on my mechanics, and stamina, and endurance, and after four months, I was able to run one hundred meters without stopping to walk.

That was definitely a *Chariots of Fire* moment: the wind whipping my hair, my arms raised above my head, smiling at the sun. My gait is different than the guys in the movie, obviously, but in my mind, I moved as smoothly as Grete Waitz. It felt like my body was working as one, part animal, part machine, fluid and slick. Suddenly, I had a goal and a purpose, a world I could embrace outside of my school and my family. Track gave me a place where I could at once fit in and escape.

For the first time in my life, I felt like I was whole.

※

When I was twelve, Paddy took me to my first track meet, the New York State Games for the Physically Challenged, at Hofstra University, an annual event that offers swimming, track and field, and other events for kids with disabilities. In this meet, we were all divvied up by disability category: Amputees raced amputees; the blind raced the blind; the wheelchairs raced the wheelchairs. (That may seem like an obvious way to set up the races, but as I came to learn a few years later, this isn't always the case.) I looked at the competitors in my track heat and thought, *How cool! Everybody's missing a leg just like me!* Paddy took a group of us amputees from the tristate area, so it was a whole weekend of hanging out with amputee kids my age.

The first night in the dorms, we girls stayed up all night and swapped hospital stories. My new friend Tammy had one of her legs amputated and was going to have her second leg amputated. And then there was Michele, who lost her leg to cancer and shared lots of horrible stories about chemo, making it sound like the amputation was the easy part.

Each of these girls was about the same age as me; they also went to schools where they were the only ones who wore prosthetic legs, and suddenly I realized I wasn't alone in the world. We talked about what names we were called in school, or what we did when we were having a "bad leg day." It was wonderful to bond with these girls, to share what I never had the chance to talk about with my old friends at school. Paddy later told me, "This wasn't only about getting you to a track meet. It was about giving you the opportunity to have other kids like you to talk to."

I ran two races at the meet, the 60m dash and the 100m dash. The 60m came first, and in the last ten meters of the race I felt the strap on my leg snap, and the leg started slipping off. I grabbed the strap and held my leg on for dear life as I outran the boy in the next lane to snag the win! I also won the 100m, again beating a few boys. And this wasn't like the Special Olympics, where everybody got a medal; there was only gold, silver, and bronze. After the meet, I thought, *I don't suck. Actually, I'm pretty good. This is very, very cool. Let's see how far I can take this.*

That afternoon, Paddy told us all about the Paralympic Games. The Paralympics are for elite athletes with disabilities, and more than one hundred countries around the world compete. They're held every four years in the same country and venue as the regular Olympics, and you compete within your own disability category. *Holy crap,* I thought, *I can go to the Olympics.* That's something I never even bothered dreaming about. After all, don't Mary Lou Retton and Joan Benoit Samuelson have two legs? Hell, I never thought that I could be an athlete, let alone an Olympian.

I wanted in.

When I told Paddy about my Paralympic goal, she pointed at my Barbie leg and said, "Fine, but that won't cut it. You need to be moving on something else." That was the first time I learned I had prosthetic options.

Paddy introduced my family to a prosthetist named Mike Joyce. Mike worked with her at NYU Hospital but had his own practice on the side, which, for political reasons, he had to keep on the down-low, so he'd see patients only at night at a little office I called "The Leg Shack," in honor of the B-52s' song "Love Shack." The Leg Shack was a three-room building in Queens, and it was a small, magic operation. Mike made me my first high-tech prosthetic leg, with a flexible suction socket (no more pinching belt around my waist . . . yay!), and my first Flex-Foot, an energy storing foot that helps give you a bounce in your step, making it easier to walk and run.

The ripple effect of meeting Paddy was huge: I had a role model, I had information, I had a place to get a better leg, and I had an Olympic-sized dream.

I started seeing David three times a week, and by now he was having me do more than run. I lifted weights, and did the Stairmaster, the rowing machine, and the stationary bike. After a good day at the gym, after doing hundreds of bicep curls, and tricep curls, and toe raises, I'd check myself out in the mirror, and think, *I'm getting kind of buff here . . . and I'm liking it. Look at those arms. Look at those legs. I'm a badass.*

Digging my new body, I decided that I wasn't ever going to allow myself to get down about the fact that I was missing a leg; I would make sure that every other part of my body would always be as strong and tough as possible. I was on the precipice of adolescence, and being a badass helped make me feel whole. For the first time in my life, I was comfortable in my own skin . . . or at least for the most part. You see, thirteen-year-old girls are *never* completely at ease, especially when they hate the way they look in all of their clothes.

Skirts were a problem for me. I never felt good wearing them because my legs were so different—and not just different from everybody else's, but from each other. The skin tone of my Barbie leg didn't match my regular leg, and the shapes were radically different, especially after I started working out, because the prosthetic leg didn't have any muscle curves.

Shoes were an issue, too. I couldn't wear high heels, because my fake foot was a hard rubber thing that pointed out at about a 90-degree angle. I could only wear flats or sneakers, not quite the dream shoe attire of a young girl.

In terms of fashion, my new Mike Joyce leg didn't help matters either, even though it looked better than the Barbie leg. It was covered with hard foam, which was covered by a geriatric stocking, and the whole thing got incredibly dirty, incredibly quickly. And during the summer, well, suffice it to say it doesn't breathe particularly well. It was also fairly wide, and not particularly girly, because it was unisex. (Actually, Mike just told us they were unisex. The fact is, these prosthetics were made for men. We women just had to accept and deal with it.) It was more comfortable than Barbie, but it still looked awful, and that was a problem, because looks were increasingly important to me.

So I figured I could either try to hide the leg, or I could live with it and try not to care what people thought—or at least pretend that I didn't care. One day I woke up, glared at the stocking-covered foam, and thought, *You know what? The raw metal might be better than this damn stocking. And it's not like what I have now is fooling anybody, so why not lose it?* So I got a pair of scissors and cut the foam right off. It looked raw, and modern and cool—I liked the shiny metal, and oddly enough, it seemed more real than the flesh-toned stocking—and I was satisfied with my handiwork. It was a pivotal, burning-of-the-bra kind of moment. For the first time, I truly owned my disability. I was proud of my body . . . even the metal parts.

My seventh grade English teacher was named Mrs. Roberts, and she was a little off kilter. She was flighty and ditzy, and people around the school theorized that she was an alcoholic. Her hair was dyed black black black, and she wore it in a bouffant. She always had on old lady lipstick and very bright clothing—purples, pinks, reds—and she had an old-school Jackie O quality . . . but far tackier.

One day in March, I didn't complete an English essay, a rarity for me, but we'd had a particularly hairy week at home, so I wasn't as focused as usual. Dad had had a bunch of meltdowns that week; he was getting ready for a big performance with his choir, and you didn't want to be near him when there was a performance around the corner. Having the snot kicked out of me multiple times, and crying so hard that I couldn't catch my breath each night, took its toll, and I simply couldn't write the essay.

Mrs. Roberts kept me after class to find out what had happened. In the past, when Dad's rage kept me from doing something—completing a school assignment, going on a playdate with a friend, whatever—I always had an excuse. But this time, I had nothing. I didn't know what to say, probably because I was so beaten down.

I told Mrs. Roberts, "Look, I just couldn't get it done. Things got a little crazy at my house last night. My Dad loses his temper sometimes." I tried to make it sound like it wasn't a big deal, but as soon as I said it, I realized my family's dirty secret was out. I thought, *Shit, I tattled on Dad. Maybe if I tell Mrs. Roberts we're taking care of it, she won't get freaked out, and she won't say anything to anybody.* "But he's getting help," I blurted. "He's going up to visit our grandparents in New Hampshire, and he's seeing a counselor up there. It'll be okay. Don't worry about it." All lies. He wasn't getting help. There was no counselor. It wasn't going to be okay.

When a teacher hears even a whiff of the possibility of child abuse, the law requires that she report it. I didn't know that. Mrs. Roberts said, "Fine, Sarah, don't worry, just get the paper to me by the end of the week. Don't you have play practice right now?" I nodded. She said, "Okay. Go ahead."

I'd landed the role of Sally in the school production of the Charlie Brown musical opus called *Snoopy!!!* (What with my blonde hair, I was a shoo-in.) I had plenty of lines, and a solo singing feature, and it was blissful to be somebody else for a few hours a day.

After we were done, Mom met me outside the rehearsal room. She gave me a hug and said, "You looked great up there, honey. Good work. Now we need to go see Principal Springer."

I asked, "The principal? What for?" I had no idea why—I was never in trouble at school. Could it be because of one measly late essay? Mom didn't seem like herself. I started to get worried.

"I'm not sure," she said. "I ran into him when I got here, and he asked me to have both of us come see him after you were done here." She avoided eye contact, which only made me more nervous.

We went to Principal Springer's office and sat down in front of his desk. He was quiet for almost a minute, then said, "Sarah, we've had a report of child abuse at your house. I need to verify that with you." He didn't mince his words; he just came out with it.

Even with my backtracking, Mrs. Roberts tattled. The cat was out of the bag. I looked at my mom, and she looked like she was fighting back the tears. I put my head down and said, "Yeah, it's true."

He looked at my mom. "Mrs. Reinertsen?"

She was crying, so all she could do was nod.

"Okay," he said, "we have to alert the state. I'm going to file the paperwork immediately. They're going to send a social worker to your home, and they're going to interview the family, and they're going to make an evaluation, and you have to abide by whatever decision they make. We don't know what's going to happen. Mr. Reinertsen might be removed from the house, but nothing will be decided for sure until the social worker finishes their evaluation. And Sarah, you can stop by my office anytime you need anything."

On the way home, Mom said, "I'm so sorry I let it go for this long. I let it get to the point where you had to tell. I let you down. It's okay. I'm glad you told. Things need to change. I just feel awful that I didn't stop it earlier." It was nice of her to apologize, but I still felt terrible for tattling. And I was having a freakout about what might happen to our family. *What if the state makes my Dad leave the house? Did I just ruin our lives?*

Dad was teaching piano lessons that night until 8:00 p.m., so we had a couple of hours before he'd get the news. I went up to my room, hid, did my homework, and went to bed early. It had been a rough day, so I had no trouble falling asleep.

It was the proverbial elephant in the room, a topic that nobody dared broach, until a couple weeks later, when a New York State social worker came to our house and interviewed us one by one. She was petite, blonde, a very normal-looking lady, well put together, very kind, not at all disheveled like your stereotypical TV-portrayed social worker. She asked us to describe the abuse: how much, how often, what kind of physical, what kind of verbal. It was a short interview, but it seemed to go on forever.

Two days later, she came back and gave us her evaluation. "I don't see any immediate threat," she said. "Your lives aren't in danger. There haven't been any broken bones, so I don't need to have Don removed." I was relieved, because despite all of the ugliness, I still would've felt awful if Dad was banished from the kingdom. I loved him, and although I didn't like his temper, I didn't want him to leave.

The social worker was right—our lives weren't in danger . . . but our emotional stability most certainly was, and once I got over the shame and embarrassment, I realized that blowing the whistle was one of the best things that had ever happened to me. We'd endured enough tension and rage.

The State mandated we attend group family therapy, and that Dad go to an additional weekly therapy meeting at a support group for abusive men. Our therapist was named Pat, and she was a huge source of support for me and my family for almost eight years. The first year, we spent most of our sessions venting, getting all the ugliness out of our systems; the real work didn't start until year two. We then learned the tools to communicate in a healthier way, to speak in sentences that started with, "It really hurts me when you . . . " rather than, "Don't fucking talk to me that way!"

Junkies can't always break their habits right away, and to me, abuse is another addiction, so I wasn't surprised that Dad couldn't stop cold turkey. The physical punishments ceased, but he continued to tell us that we never did anything right—he got on Peter constantly about the lawn: "You missed a spot. Can't you do anything right?" But now, when he started to lose it, we were hip enough to say, "Dad, you're crossing the line. Pull yourself together."

We slowly seemed to heal as a unit, and I began to think that maybe, just maybe we could become that perfect family the outside world had once believed us to be.

CHAPTER 2

BECOMING A CHAMPION

In August of 1988, when I turned thirteen, I was eligible to participate in my first international track meet, the Canadian National Championships in Calgary. The 1988 Seoul Paralympics were happening that same summer, so I was a bit bummed that I was too young to try out for the team—the minimum age to be a Paralympian was sixteen—but Calgary was a great place to kick off my international track career. I knew the Paralympics would come eventually.

My first race was the 100m. All the other racers were older—the youngest one was a twenty-three-year-old medical school student—so I was unbelievably intimidated. Yeah, I was fast, and yeah, I qualified at the U.S. Nationals, but I was still a rookie who had no idea if her little legs would move quickly enough to beat the big girls.

Turns out they would.

I had a great race, so great that I crossed the line in a time that eclipsed the world record. I waited by the track while the officials determined whether or not my time was wind aided. And I waited. And waited. And waited. After what seemed like six hours, but was in reality about six minutes, it was determined that, yes, I had officially broken the world record. The record time wasn't that impressive by today's standards—we're talking twenty-three-some-odd seconds, and I did it in twenty-one-plus—so I had improved by almost two seconds. I was happy, but far from satisfied. I'd only been training for a year, and I'd put up better times in practice, so I knew there was plenty of room to improve. (To give you some perspective about how far things have progressed both in terms of training and hardware, as of this writing, disabled racers are regularly running the 100m in about seventeen seconds.) The 200m race was held later that day, and it was more of the same: the gun, the run, the wait, the record. Two gold medals, two world records. I was on my way.

Two years later, it was off to St. Etienne, France, for the Junior World Disabled Championships, a meet that featured the world's best under-twenty-one disabled athletes. My brother and both of my parents came with me this time, and for all practical purposes, this was our family vacation. As was usually the case, it wasn't a *real* vacation—it was going somewhere to watch Sarah run again—but it was important nonetheless, because traveling was one of the things that held the family together. We had our dark secret about the rage and fighting that went on at home with our dad, but these trips, these track meets, were some of our happiest times as a family. We united around the sport, and the sport united us.

The one notable difference between Calgary and St. Etienne was that the women's field was small and disorganized. This wasn't uncommon, because at this point, there weren't as many disabled girl runners as there were boys, partly because many foreign doctors convinced their team coaches that girls shouldn't run on the prosthetic legs, as it posed a greater risk to them than men. At some meets, there were so few women signed up that my races were cancelled altogether.

A lot of people had come a long way to be in France, and everybody wanted the race to happen, so the race officials had to get creative, and in this case, getting creative meant combining all the women's disability classifications. Normally, they divvy us up not just by categories, but by subcategories: Above-the-knee amputees raced against above-the-knee amputees, below-the-knees raced against below-the-knees, and so forth. But with this new paradigm, I was racing against some people who had cerebral palsy, and some who had amputated arms, and some who had amputated legs. It was like they told us, *Everybody in the pool! If you're a female racer, and you have a disability of any kind, get to the starting line.*

It wasn't a fair race—it was kind of a stupid race when you think about it—but at least there *was* a race. (This sort of thing continued to be a problem for over a decade; as recently as 2004, female classifications were similarly combined at the Paralympics. This is part of the reason why I don't run short distance track anymore. It became next to impossible to recruit other women to race, because how can you tell somebody that there was a chance that they'd train for four years and end up racing against people who are considerably more and/or less abled than them?) I was a bit intimidated to run against some of the girls with two legs, but I didn't let it stop me from kicking ass, and I wound up coming in second place, something I always counted as one of my proudest finishes. I mean, beating a two-legged runner? It couldn't get much better than that.

✳

I had a lot of different interests in high school—sports, listening to punk music, writing in my journal—so I never felt pressured to hang out with one circle of people. I ended up floating from clique to clique, not *in* groups, but *of* groups. A good example: I was in the orchestra, but I wasn't a music geek. Violin was fulfilling and fun, but it wasn't even close to the singular focal point of my life.

That said, track was at the top of the list, because when I ran, none of the superficial high school crap mattered. I spent many after-school hours training with a bunch of guys from the U.S. Disabled Track Team, like a below-knee amputee named Dennis Oehler, and above-knee amputee Todd Schaffhauser. They were the world record holders respectively in the 100m and 200m dash, and they both lived on Long Island, about forty-five minutes away. Dennis and Todd were both in their thirties, but they all but ignored our age difference; besides, we were all training for the 1992 Paralympic Games in Barcelona, and since we all had the same goals, age didn't matter.

I related well to adults partly because I'd been dealing with adult issues for virtually my entire life, like coping with the loss of a limb, or trying to find a sense of identity, or trying to ignore the phantom pain that kept me awake night after night after night, or figuring out how to keep my father from beating the crap out of me and Peter. Being the only kid in my 1,500-person high school with a disability lent itself to a lot of soul searching, the kind of soul searching that'll make you grow up fast. I couldn't help but become more mature.

Sometimes being a grown-up adolescent was counterproductive. I was always articulate and could speak on an adult level, which sometimes made me come off as a know-it-all, a teacher's pet, a person who took classes a bit too seriously. If I'm being honest, I suppose I *was* a bit of a know-it-all. I always raised my hand to answer the questions and volunteered for extra credit, something that doesn't always enamor one to the rest of the class. It took me a while to realize that I'd be better off picking my spots, even if it meant dumbing myself down once in a while.

Dumbing down was hard, though, because my brain never stopped working. I was always a voracious reader, and after I made it through the Judy Blumes and the Beverly Clearys and C. S. Lewis books of the world, I went on to more adult books, literature that wasn't necessarily for my age group, like V. C. Andrews and Stephen King. Fortunately, Mom and Dad never censored my reading material. One of the first adult titles I checked out—and we're talking fifth grade, here—was *Dianetics* by L. Ron Hubbard. It wasn't that I had any particular interest in Scientology; I picked it up because the local TV stations played the *Dianetics* commercial over and over and over again, so when I stumbled across it at a bookstore, I thumbed through it, and thought, *I should see what this is all about.* (Eleven years old, and checking out *Dianetics*—Cruise and Travolta would've been proud.) I read the whole thing, not because I enjoyed it, but just so I could say I made it to the end. My thirst for words wasn't limited to books; Dad had a subscription to *Time,* which I pored through every week, from cover to cover. Some kids like cartoons. I liked news.

School and learning didn't come as easily to Peter, and the fact that he was living in the shadow of an older sister who always got good grades made matters even worse. This was one of the many things that helped shape our, shall we say, *interesting* family dynamic. I required more attention from my parents because of my medical issues, and that was rough on Peter. He was angry and frustrated, and often told my parents something along the lines of, "It's not fair that she gets to do so much more than I do all because she's missing her leg!" Fortunately, he never took it out on me.

Dealing with the media also aged me pretty quickly.

I was invited to be featured in a book by Kurt Vonnegut's then-wife, photographer Jill Krementz. Jill had gotten in touch with Paddy Rossbach to discuss a book she was working on called *How It Feels to Live with a Physical*

Disability, and was looking for kids to photograph and interview. Paddy immediately thought of me and hooked me up
with Jill, who conducted an interview/photo session at our
home in Huntington Bay.

Once the book hit the streets, I did several interviews
to promote it, including an appearance on Maury Povich's
talk show. I was kind of psyched about the whole thing, not
because I had any burning desire to be on television, but
rather because I got to miss a day of school.

Mom bought me a nice black blazer-shirt-and-skirt set
at my favorite clothing store, the Rexer-Parkes boutique in
downtown Huntington. Since I'd be wearing a skirt, I chose
to wear my more realistic-looking prosthetic leg—that was
the one encased in foam—covered with a pair of stockings.
That's how all the television anchor ladies dressed, so I figured, *Why not me?*

I knew what Maury Povich's show was about, so I guess
it shouldn't have surprised me that when I got to the studio, the dweeby, skinny, bespectacled producer came into
the green room and said, "Love your outfit. You look great.
But Maury wanted me to ask if you'd go out into the studio
without your leg on."

I was horrified. *Horrified.*

I looked the dweeb right in the eye and said, "I'm wearing a nice new outfit here. What do you want me to do, rip
off my stockings and then take off my leg?" It was cheap
and made me feel like I was coming from a circus sideshow.
I hated taking my leg off in front of people; even now, I

generally only do when I'm taking a shower, or before I'm going to bed, or switching legs during a triathlon. But to do it in a television studio just so I could sit there and look more disabled for Maury Povich? Screw that.

I held my ground, and the dweeb smiled and said, "Okay, okay, fine, fine," but I could tell he was thinking, *Damn, she didn't take it off. There goes our Money Shot.* It was my first glimpse at how slimy and lowbrow the media could be.

All that said, the interview went very well, I gave strong answers and even made everyone laugh, and it certainly helped my stature around school. I went from being somewhat of an outsider, to somewhat of a cool kid. I wasn't ever going to win any of those yearbook contests—Most Popular, Most Likely to Succeed, Most Athletic—but I had my own deal going, and I reveled in it.

❈

People have always stared at me, but when I hit teenagehood, my senses were heightened to the gawking, and I knew I had to develop a Zen way of dealing with it, or I'd go nuts. My mom had always explained that most people stared not because they were mean, but only because they were curious. She was right, but it still didn't make it any easier to take. I tried to remind myself that curiosity could lead to new knowledge and understanding, so when kids gawked, I often preemptively asked them, "Do you have any questions for me?" And that would often lead to them asking me how I lost my leg, or why I have to wear that metal leg. But other days I would just throw on a pair of sunglasses and block out the stares and avoid the eye contact altogether.

When I wasn't able to compartmentalize, or if I was in a bad mood, I'd tell whoever was checking me out that I'd lost my leg in a parachuting accident or a shark attack. (Shark attacks are cool. Proximal femoral focal deficiency isn't.) I also went through an aggressive New Yorker phase, and for about eight months, if I caught somebody peering at my leg, I'd look them right in the eye and say, *"Stare much? Whatcha looking at? Didn't your Mom teach ya any manners?"* Usually it would shame them into looking away, but that sort of behavior wasn't the least bit constructive for anybody. I wasn't owning my prosthetic . . . but I had to amuse myself, and sometimes I couldn't take people just staring unabashedly. I was a tough little girl, but tough little girls can't be tough all the time.

Once I got past my aggro period, I tried to use humor to make people feel comfortable. When you're the person who's sort of different—when you're The Other—oftentimes it's your job to make everybody else feel okay about you . . . and that's not particularly fair, is it?

None of these tactics really helped me deal with boys. Especially boys like Brad Shoemaker.

A teenybopper cutie from the wrestling team, Brad was acknowledged to be one of the cooler kids in my freshman class. He wasn't the smartest guy in class, but his innate sweetness made up for it, plus he made me laugh, which counted for a lot. We dated for a while—if you could call talking on the phone for two hours every night dating—and had a great time. We passed notes in the hallway, and met in between classes, and kissed in front of our lockers, and as inexperienced kissers, our kisses often involved bumped foreheads and crashed teeth. I was a freshman in high school and I thought that finally, I had a real boyfriend, and it was about time.

Two months into couplehood, out of nowhere, Brad turned mean. He cut our phone calls short and refused to meet me at my locker. And then, also out of nowhere, he broke up with me. In the hallway. In between classes. And it was cold: "I don't really like you anymore. Let's not go out." Then the bell rang and he dashed off to class. I stood there, bewildered as to what exactly went wrong and why he didn't like me anymore. It was a total blindsiding. I mean, getting dumped by the jock wrestler kid, and in public yet? Come *on*.

The following week, my friend Whitney—whose boyfriend was on the wrestling team with Brad—wandered over to my locker and said, "I think I know why Brad broke up with you."

"Yeah? Why?"

"The other guys on the team were talking shit about him because he was dating you. He told me they were saying stuff like, 'What's it like to fuck a one-legged girl?'"

"Shut *up*."

"Yeah. For a while he was like, 'I find *both* of her legs kind of sexy.' But I think he got tired of it."

I know she was trying to make me feel better about the whole thing—or at least help me understand what had happened—but the only thing it did was make me realize that a lot of people looked at me as damaged goods.

Brad was not the man of my dreams, but it seemed that losing him meant losing the only boy in the whole school who would even dare to go out with me. If he couldn't handle it, how could I expect any of the high school boys to be any different? My mom always comforted me in these moments by saying, "Sarah, obviously Brad wasn't the quality guy you deserve, and if they're not strong enough to handle your leg, they're not the kind of guy you want to go out with." I knew that was true, but it still didn't make me feel any better. I was alone, the leper in school who would never have a boyfriend until college, when boys might be mature enough to ask me out.

❋

I started hanging out with the older punk kids at school when I was a freshman, partly because I liked their taste in music—Fugazi, Gorilla Biscuits, Bad Religion, and especially Rollins Band—and partly because of the outsider factor. (Always being an outsider, always being The Other, was the reality of my fifteen-year-old, Long Island world.)

Admittedly, I wasn't as punk as they were: I never dyed my hair purple, or red, or green, and I was too young and too chickenshit to get a tattoo. Besides, taking my prosthetic into account, I felt like I already had my version of a tattoo; it was an imprint that wouldn't go away. My new friends were freaks by choice, but I was at home with them because I often felt like The Other, too. They welcomed me with open arms. They were my haven.

David McLean was on the periphery of that group. My crush on David kicked in when he was a senior, and I was a sophomore. David played drums in the marching band, as well as in a rock group called Down Time. I played violin in the orchestra. David was a punk kid trapped in the body of a preppie. I was an amputee runner who rolled with the hardcore punks. Match made in heaven, right?

I'd known about David for a while, but I didn't start thinking about him as potential boyfriend material until the homecoming dance that October. David didn't look or act like the rest of my crowd. He was a classic, all-American boy who always did what his parents told him to do, always tried to do the right thing. He took sailing lessons at a yacht club and graduated at the top of his class, but he also smoked cigarettes and played in that punk band. Music and Marlboro Reds were his form of rebellion.

My sophomore homecoming dance was the first high school dance I ever went to; I didn't get to go freshman year because no boy asked me, and I was too scared to show up by myself. That year I went with a bunch of my friends—David included—and having them by my side gave me the confidence to be at the party without a date. Before the dance, we all pre-gamed in my friend Rob's VW van, and by the time we made our way inside the Huntington High School gym (home of the Blue Devils, by the way), we were all a little tipsy.

We danced with abandon when they put on Depeche Mode, Jane's Addiction, Prince, or Violent Femmes, and we ran off the floor screaming in horror when they played Def Leppard, Vanilla Ice, or MC Hammer. We moved to the music as one big organism, but David and I danced together separately. (Okay, we only danced together *sort of* separately—it was hard to completely break off from the group.) David was a great partner because he had no fear— he just *moved*. He wasn't like a lot of other boys at my school who would only dance when they were drunk. David was this uninhibited guy who loved to boogie, yet another reason he was so desirable. I tried to position myself directly in front of him, and whenever I managed to get him at just the right angle, it felt to me like we were almost a couple. It was our secret moment, our *Sixteen Candles* moment, my chance to dance with Jake Ryan.

It didn't surprise us when David got nominated for homecoming king. All of us punks voted for him, but apparently a whole lot of other people did too, because the guy won. That's part of the reason I knew there was no chance of hooking up with him that night. The spotlight was on him. For the rest of the night, he *was* Jake Ryan. As he did the obligatory dance with the homecoming queen, I hung out with my fellow Others and admired him from afar.

But I wanted him a-near. I just didn't know how to make it happen. So, as was often the case when I had problems, I turned to *Seventeen*.

I subscribed to *Seventeen* magazine, and when it showed up in the mail each month, I'd study each glossy page, trying to become a strong girl-slash-woman. But since all the models in there were perfect—perfect hair, perfect shoes, perfect bodies—I wasn't sure where I fit in. Also, it didn't really give me help in figuring out how to make David mine, so I came up with my own plan: Admit to one of my friends I liked him.

Talking about my feelings was also a calculated move; I figured once I voiced them, it would somehow get back to David, and the lines of communication would magically open. I knew he wouldn't open them himself, because when it came to girls, David was pretty clueless. I could have worn a shirt that said, "I HAVE A CRUSH ON DAVID MCLEAN" and he probably still wouldn't have realized that I liked him. Since it was getting close to his graduation, I figured I'd better make some semblance of a move before it was too late.

Good thing Rob was having one of his notorious get-togethers.

Rob's parents used to go out of town a whole bunch, so he always had great parties, in part because he had a nice area in his basement where Down Time could play.

Another plus was that Rob lived close to me, which meant there was a better chance I'd be able to sneak back home after my 12:30 curfew without getting grounded.

David looked and played great that night, and I was more into him than ever, if that was possible. At 11:00, after the cops came by and told the band to pull the plug, everybody broke off into couples and slipped into different rooms throughout Rob's house to do who knew what. I wandered out to the patio, and plopped down and spread out on a big lounge chair. Eventually, David came over and sat down across the table from me, and we looked up at the stars, and we talked. And talked. And talked. He was a smart guy, and we discussed books we'd read in our English classes, and our respective philosophies of life, and who our favorite J. D. Salinger characters were, and it was incredibly hot. Good-looking guys aren't always the biggest turn-on for me—I like the smart ones. But David was both. And that's not even taking into account that he was also a preppy punk rock star.

It amazed me that, after about three or four hours of chatting together, he still didn't understand that I *liked him* liked him. I could have tried to get a little physical if our chairs weren't so damn far apart, but since we were separated by a good five feet, I didn't have the opportunity to "accidentally" brush his hand with mine, or "mistakenly" lean into his side. I wasn't the kind of bold girl who would crawl across the table and jump him. Also, I had no confidence in my ability to connect with a boy, as the last one

I had any interest in blew me off because he was tired of getting teased by his wrestling teammates about going to the movies with the one-legged girl. And besides, I was just some underclassman, and David was getting ready to graduate, and there was a good chance he didn't even think of me as more than a friend.

Monday at school, I told my friend Tania, "David's cute. I like him. A *lot*," so she made it her mission to make sure he knew, and that did it. Once he realized I was officially into him, he got into me, but if Tania hadn't said anything, there was a chance nothing would have happened, because he was *so* oblivious. (A few weeks later, I asked David, "Why do you think I sat out there at Rob's house and chatted with you for five hours, and broke my curfew, and got grounded? It was to hang out with you.")

David, of course, knew all about my leg, because he was kinda-sorta part of my freak circle, and this circle was always very supportive, and cool, and open about my situation, even to the point that we would make jokes about it. Like when I'd wear fishnets over the raw metal with my Doc Marten shoes, they'd say something like, *That looks so badass. Who cares that you ripped a hole in the stockings? That's how they're supposed to look.* (Punk rock fashion was sort of easy to pull off with the body that I had.) David made it clear that he had no problem with it. He respected me as a person and as an athlete. He didn't think of me as the poor crippled girl who ran track on that weird metal thing. He didn't pity me.

The next week, Rob's parents went out of town again, so guess what? Yep, another party . . . but this one was going to be an all-nighter, a sleepover. I'd told my parents that I was staying at Tania's, but in reality, I was going to crash at Rob's along with everybody else who had lied to their parents about where they were staying.

At 2:00 a.m., a few people started getting naked, and jumping into the pool, and they wanted me to join them, and I was mortified. I raced to the bathroom to escape, to come up with a game plan. I sat down on the edge of the bathtub and went into my head: *You do not want to remove your leg in front of the entire party, so what the hell are you going to do now? All these people are skinny-dipping and having fun. This is about being young and making memories. Carpe diem! Seize the day! You've been taking off your prosthetic at the beach since you were four and didn't think twice about anybody staring at you. Besides, Mom always says, "The leg always weeds out the bad ones, and if your friends are good ones, they won't care about it, they'll love you for who you are." What's the big deal? You're a strong person. You're an athlete.*

Rob, Tim, Shannon, Dale, Heather, Stacie, and the rest of the lot didn't have to psyche themselves up to take off their clothes, because they didn't have to remove an artificial limb. Once again, I was The Other.

Even more difficult to grasp was the idea of taking off my leg in front of David. If I did, it would be the first time a boy I liked would scrutinize me. This wasn't just walking anonymously down the hallway wearing jeans and a t-shirt, using my books to cover up my chest. There would be a spotlight shining on me and my leg. There was also the curiosity factor: Everybody knew I wore a prosthetic, so it was inevitable they would stare. It's human nature. I wasn't going to slip under the radar this time. It was beyond a bikini moment—and we *all* know what a bikini moment is—which is horrifying enough in and of itself. I knew every single person at that party was thinking, *What's it going to look like when she takes off the leg? I have to watch.* And the fact that I was fifteen and concerned about my flat-chested gymnast body didn't help matters.

It went beyond nudity for me. It was like I was going to be a centerfold model.

After another ten minutes of psyching myself up—or beating myself up, depending on how you look at it—I finally started to believe it would be okay to get into the pool one-legged, and if David had a problem with it, I shouldn't be with him anyhow. I left the bathroom, walked out to the backyard, sat down at a table by the swimming pool, and took a sip of liquid courage.

Then I took off my right sneaker.

Then I slipped my right leg out of my shorts.

Then I unclipped my prosthetic.

Then I slid the frame off my stump.

Then I took off the stump stock.

Then I leaned the artificial leg against the table, and draped it with a towel for protection.

Then I *didn't* take off my t-shirt and my underwear, because how naked could I really get?

Then I hopped out of the chair.

And without doing any more self-analysis, I dived into the pool.

I left the prosthetic behind, and I was free.

We splashed, and floated, and tried to open our eyes under the water. In the water, we were all equals. David played with me, and was wholly unfazed. He was comfortable with me, so *I* was comfortable with me.

An hour later, we all got out of the pool, completely soaked, and completely screwed because Rob didn't have enough towels. I was worse off than the other skinny-dippers, because my t-shirt was wet. David, gallant boy that he was, offered me his top. I offered him a kiss, then sat down and put my prosthetic back on.

After we were more or less dried off, we went upstairs, sneaked into one of the guest bedrooms, fell into the bed, and started passionately making out. I was totally in the moment . . . or *almost* totally in the moment. I couldn't let myself go completely because in the back of my head, I kept thinking, *You're going to have to take off the leg again . . . you're going to have to take off the leg again . . . you're going to have to take off the leg again. He's moving his hand across your stomach and up toward your chest, and you're going to have to take off the leg again. So when does the leg come off? Before the shirt? After the shirt? In five minutes? In ten?* There definitely weren't any articles in *Seventeen* about this sort of thing.

After a couple more minutes of fumbling around, I asked him to turn off the lights. Safely hidden in the dark, in two smooth moves, I slipped off the leg and slid under the covers, and David didn't flinch, and I was blissfully relieved. He still held me, and kissed me, and wanted me, and desired me. He passed the test. *I* passed the test. I felt adored and accepted.

That night, we slept together.

Now I don't mean sleeping together as in having sex—I mean sleeping together as in sharing the same bed. Sure, there was the making out, and the heavy petting, and it was lovely, but I wasn't ready to have sex. Unsurprisingly, David, good guy that he was, didn't pressure me. He was a virgin like I was, probably because a girl had to hit him over the head before he knew she liked him.

I know my stump isn't attractive—it's skinny and weird looking, and it has scars all over it. Even today, when I sit at the beach, I cover it up with a blanket or a towel, and if people ask why, I tell them it's to keep it out of the sun, but the simple fact is that I don't like the way it looks. But I wasn't worried that David would be grossed out. He'd seen me at the pool, and he hadn't run away, and I knew there wouldn't be any rejection.

When I told David, "Okay, I'm going to take off the leg now," it was one of the most frightening, most intimate moments of my life, but it was all more than okay, because when he held me in his arms, it was an affirmation that I could be wanted. Sports made me feel good about my body, but getting such potent reinforcement from a smart, good-looking boy in a punk band was amazing.

I woke up the next morning, and David's arms were still around me. I thought, *Wow. He didn't change his mind.*

He made me feel like I was worth as much as anybody else.

He made me feel like a whole woman.

※

I was still lusting after the 1992 Paralympic Games in Barcelona, but it wasn't only about the competition or the sport. Aside from the actual racing, I dreamed of representing the United States. Although my mother wasn't born here, she and my dad raised me and Peter to be proud of our home, to be proud of being American citizens. I was only fifteen, but I knew the importance of country.

As always, my family was 100 percent behind me, and they wanted me to achieve my dream, to reach my goal. But it soon became apparent that my parents couldn't afford to cover the cost of training, the travel, and the $3,000 fee I'd need to pay the U.S. Paralympic Team, so they sought out help.

The community rallied around us: Conrad Sump, one of the members of Dad's church choir, was an experienced fund-raiser, and set up an organization called Friends of Sarah. Conrad had some church members put together a mailing list, after which they mailed out hundreds of F.O.S.

flyers with directions as to how donors could contribute to my cause. And they cast a wide net: friends of friends, business associates of business associates. Anybody who Conrad thought would throw us some money got a flyer.

I thought the whole thing would be uncomfortable for me, like I was the creepy Long Island poster child for disabled athletes, but that wasn't at all the case. The people were behind me because they *believed,* not because they felt sorry for me, and we ended up raising over $10,000. It was a huge relief, and I felt like there was nothing stopping me now; I could afford to travel to the trials, and buy new Nike Air 180s, and some track spikes. My only job: Dream, train, run my ass off, and make the U.S. Paralympic Team.

After I finished eleventh grade, I temporarily moved out to Boulder, Colorado, so I could train full-time with David Balsley. My life was simple and regimented: Wake up, eat breakfast, take the bus to David's place, train, go home to the apartment my parents had rented for me, eat lunch, train some more, go home, eat dinner, go to sleep. I didn't have a car, and had to walk everywhere, but fortunately my two main necessities—a grocery store and hiking/running trails—were practically right around the corner. My social life was nonexistent, and aside from endless phone calls to my Long Island friends (e.g., David McLean) and periodic visits from my mother, David Balsley was the only person I interacted with on a regular basis. If I didn't have such a tangible goal, I'd have gone nuts.

I became aware of how very alone I was when I caught the worst flu in history. David came by with Saltines and ginger ale, and Mom called constantly, but I took care of myself, and made it through just fine. That was a defining moment for me. It taught me that I could manage on my own, even while suffering through nonstop puking. I knew then that I'd be ready for college, and ready for *life*.

I went to Emory University in Atlanta for the Paralympic Qualifiers. Only two women would be chosen for the U.S. track team to Barcelona, and I planned to be one of them. There was only one women's race in Spain, so the only race I focused on at that meet was the 100m dash.

In the warmups, I liked to try and psyche out my opponents, but my psyche-out method was kind of lame: I let out a few animal-like grunts. I always sort of felt like a tiger that was gearing up to jump out of the cage and run for its life, so the animal grunting seemed very natural. It got me all revved up, but it never scared anybody.

The 100m is a short race, so the start is everything. If you stumble coming out of the blocks, it's almost impossible to make up the lost time along the way, so you have to find a way to calm those nerves. (I tended to do a lot of deep breathing exercises: *in through the nose and out through the mouth, in through the nose and out through the mouth.*) And then, next thing you know, it's a mass of running legs, and pumping arms, all culminating with a lean across the finish line, and seventeen seconds later, it was done. I took home a gold medal in my division, and earned the coveted spot on the team. David also had some kind words, but then added, "Now the work really begins."

He meant it. We went right back to Colorado the very next day, and it was business as usual.

After another several weeks of training, I flew out to Madrid, and then Barcelona with the entire team, and within thirty minutes of touching down at Aeroport de Barcelona, I had an anxiety attack, because my prosthetics were still in Madrid, and wouldn't get to Barcelona for four more days. (I learned a valuable, valuable lesson: Always carry my prosthetic legs onto the plane.) I wasn't the only person on the team who got screwed. Yes, it was a charter plane, and yes, the airline knew who we were and what we were going out to Spain for, but for some unfathomable reason, they didn't account for all the extra baggage and wheelchairs.

Thanks to the fine folks at TWA, I lost two days of training, which wasn't the ideal way to prepare for the biggest race of my life. I ran in my walking leg just to loosen up my body and try and get over the jet lag, but I didn't get to really sprint like I wanted and needed to.

It wasn't a total bummer, because there was plenty to do at the spectacular Olympic Village. The Village was situated right along the Mediterranean, and I had an ocean view from my apartment suite. There was a cafeteria that was open most of the day offering buffet after buffet after buffet, and they had everything: a Kosher station, Spanish food, Mediterranean food, Chinese food, every cuisine you could imagine. And for those who couldn't deal with the healthier fare, there was a McDonald's in the Village. (I didn't indulge until after I was done with the competition.) There were arcade rooms, a hair salon, and chill-out lounges. It was like the coolest college campus ever.

There were cute boy athletes all over the place, and after a summer with David Balsley, I was like a kid in a candy store. I developed several crushes, most notably on a volleyball player named Dave Newkirk. He was 6'4", handsome, smart, and on his way to an engineering degree, a total catch. He had a prosthetic arm that allowed him to bump the volleyball unbelievably well, and was one of the team's key players. We would have dinner together back at the athletes' village, and when I wasn't racing or training I would watch the U.S. volleyball games. Dave and I lived in different states, so I knew the relationship wasn't going anywhere, but it was just fun to have a crush at the games, and we could relate to each other well because of our disabilities and mutual interest in sports. He wasn't The One, but he was a good one nonetheless.

Not all the athletes were cool and cute. The crazy Russian runners and nutty German jumpers, for instance, sucked on cigarettes right out in the middle of the Olympic Village. Apparently smoking was expected, because there were ashtrays adorned with the Paralympic logo in all the suites. I eventually learned that Spain was all about smoking—you could puff anywhere, from the subway, to a restaurant, to the bank—so they probably assumed since they all lusted after tobacco, we all lusted after tobacco. (They were stingy with the towels—we only got one each—but generous with the ashtrays. I'm not sure what that says about Spain, but there it is.)

Four days before the race, we learned that, as was the case in France, there weren't going to be enough women to fill the arm amputee field and a leg amputee field, so the classifications would be combined. Just like that, I went from being a world record holder with huge expectations to win a medal to being one of the most disadvantaged people in the race. There was no way a girl with one leg and two arms could possibly beat a well-trained female athlete with two legs and one arm. What was supposed to be an equal opportunity event turned out to be an unfairly weighted fiasco.

I also felt for all the other girls, because I thought we women were being marginalized. The questions flew: Hadn't they gathered registrations before we arrived? Why didn't they know until just before the race that they'd have to combine us? How would we get more leg amputee women to race and build up our numbers, if this was what they had to contend with?

The coaches tried to put a positive spin on the situation, telling us, "Just be happy you get to run at all." That didn't make me feel any better. I thought about the hours and hours and hours I'd worked for this, and now, for reasons completely out of my hands, the odds were stacked big-time against me. My race was done before it even started.

The outcome was decided. The weeks I'd lived in Colorado, and the money that my family had spent, and the donations from the Friends of Sarah were all for naught. But there was nothing we could do. It was what it was.

David told me, "You know what? You can focus on setting another world record in your category. All the international judges are here, and all the drug testers are here, and if the wind isn't a factor, you can do it." That was a good carrot—a world record would've softened the blow—but there wasn't going to be a medal unless all the other girls twisted their ankles.

At the semifinal heat, I was distracted, ultranervous, and psyched out by the two-legged girls on either side of me, which is probably why I stumbled onto the track coming out of the starting blocks. (This wasn't unprecedented. I tripped periodically during starts, because it's difficult to keep squared off and hold a set position at the starting line with a prosthetic leg.) I finished second-to-last and didn't even make the finals, and that was it. That was my big Paralympic moment. I gave it my best, but I couldn't pull through under the strange, messed-up circumstances. It was devastating. It killed my spirit. I thought, *What's the point? Why follow the rules? Why bother at all?* My dreams went down the crapper, and my motivation was close behind.

The Games weren't covered on television, so when I got home, I had to rehash the story time and again. Dozens of people had given hundreds of dollars to help me get to the games, and I couldn't pull through, and I felt like I'd let them down. Of course nobody said I let them down; in fact everyone was a bit outraged that the Paralympic organizers had done this to me. Their outpouring of support was nice, but it didn't make up for my broken heart.

Eventually, I got tired of relating the complete story over, and over, and over again, so I started telling people I tripped at the starting line and didn't mention the combined classifications. Everybody was sympathetic, but that didn't make me feel any better, because my dream, the shining North Star of my life, was over.

For the first time in my life, I didn't really have a goal. I spent a whole lot of time thinking, *Now what?*

❈

Meanwhile, back on the home front, we were all working diligently to repair our broken family, and Dad seemed to be making progress. But senior year in high school, soon after we came back from Barcelona, things started to unravel, and it happened *fast*. Dad started blowing off our sessions with the therapist, which pissed us all off, because, as I told him, "We're in this therapy because of you, Don." (Calling him by his first name had become a regular thing. It was one of my ways to fight his authority. Petty, but effective.) His excuses were lame, like, *Things had gotten crazy at school,* or *We had a late rehearsal.* We figured he just didn't want to be there, because it was difficult for him to deal with self-examination. Turned out he wasn't showing up for reasons that were far worse.

One afternoon, Peter was downtown, and ran into his friend John. John asked, "Dude, is your aunt in town? I saw her and Don at the Greek diner late last night, like around midnight."

Peter said, "My aunt? What did this lady look like?"

John shrugged. "She was a blonde lady. I figured she was just another one of those blonde Reinertsens."

Peter said, "My aunt isn't in town."

John said, "Oh." What else could he say?

The minute Peter got home, he gave me the news. I asked, "What's Dad doing at a diner at midnight with a woman who isn't our mother?"

"I don't know." We decided we would ask him about it at our next therapy session. And once we did, it all blew up. Dad was seeing another woman. This was the first Mom was hearing any of this, and it crushed her.

Peter and I, however, weren't crushed; we were pissed. Five years of therapy, shot to hell. He wasn't just cheating on my mom, he was cheating on *everybody*. We were all in therapy, because of *his* temper, *his* rage, and now he was leaving us for an entirely new family. Unreal.

Shortly after that session, Dad decided to move out. We tried to convince him to stay and work on our family, but he was done. Right before Christmas, he rented an apartment in Centerport, and he planned to leave for good in January. I insisted that we break the news to our extended family—my grandparents, as well as some aunts, uncles, and cousins—on Christmas Day, because there was no way I'd allow us to pretend we were the perfect family ever again, especially on Christmas. I refused to sit around the dinner table and make believe that everything was all *la-di-da.*

I told Dad, "Either you're going to tell them, or I'm going to tell them, and I don't think you'll like how I'd do it. Make a decision: me or you."

He wisely said, "Okay. I'll do it."

After dinner and before dessert, I herded everybody in the family room for a special family meeting. Nobody spoke, so I broke the ice by saying, "Well we've gathered you for a reason. Dad has something to tell you."

And with that, Dad stood up and said that he was leaving. He was very meek about the whole thing. My grandparents looked shocked, especially my grandmother. Her mouth dropped open and the blood seemed to run out of her face. Once my grandfather got his bearings, he threw us a lot of questions, all of which were along the lines of, *Does he really have to move out?* He asked if there was another solution, if there was anything that he could do to help?

Dad said that he needed some space; he mostly stared at the floor, clearly uncomfortable, but steady in his resolve. And with that, it was time for dessert. On paper that seems like a weird way to go about it—drop the bomb first, eat Christmas cookies second—but it was for the best.

For years, I'd subconsciously known that the separation was coming, but now that it was real, it was devastating. My parents' marriage was over, and I felt the earth crumble beneath my feet. I'd lost at the Paralympics, so my identity as an athlete was skewed, and now my family was disintegrating. Yes, we'd been screwed up for a while, but the fact that everybody in the outside world looked at us as the perfect unit—the blonde hair, the sunny dispositions, the little amputee girl who'd overcome so much—made me feel that someday, we really could become the perfect unit.

But it was over. We were finally done protecting our Dad, and projecting the illusion of a tight family. Our heads were out of the sand. We could breathe. We were free.

CHAPTER 3

EVEN THE BEST RUNNERS CAN'T RUN AWAY

C apitol Health wasn't a job. It was a salvation.

Since money was tight in our house, I didn't get an allowance from either of my parents, and not because they didn't want to give it to me, but because they couldn't afford it. So if I wanted spending money I had to get a job. And I needed spending money, because I had a music habit to take care of; there was always a new record by The Cure, David Bowie, Midnight Oil, Madonna, Michael Jackson, or Depeche Mode that needed to be added to the collection.

And of course, I had to have my clothes. My parents bought me plenty of outfits, but it wasn't enough for the insatiable fashion appetite of a teenage girl from Long Island. I couldn't afford expensive duds, so I scoured the Salvation Army or the local thrift shops to find cool, unique gear, and I cruised the outlet stores for deep discounts. I tried to make my dollar go as far as possible—especially if I wanted some cash left over for a slice of pizza and movie tickets on the weekend.

I fit right in at Capitol Health, because all the other employees were my people: freaks. My friend Tania—who actually got me the job during my sophomore year—was one of the head freaks, and she dyed her hair on a weekly basis; sometimes it was green, sometimes it was purple, then it would be fire engine red. (Despite her surface freakiness, Tania transcended social groups—she was in the orchestra, and took AP classes, and related to everybody—and was elected class president.) And then there was Lisa, who had a nose piercing and tattoos, and the eternally sweet and adorable, but tough-looking Shane, with his shaved head, and his black leather jacket, and his Doc Marten boots. And there was Steve the hippie owner, who looked like a skinny Jerry Garcia, what with his big beard and long dark ponytail, and Steve's wife Judith, with her Birkenstock sandals and radical feminist views. (Steve and Judith had three kids, and their family seemed to be the perfectly peaceful unit, something I wished I had.)

Part of the reason I loved Capitol was that I felt like my metal leg and limping walk didn't draw as much attention as the punk-rock tattooed purple-haired girl working the juice bar. They were all so different, and I felt like my difference melted into the background. I was just another one of the cast of characters in the store. I wasn't the only freak, and it was such a comforting place to come to after a day at high school; even though it was work, I didn't care, I just loved being there with my crew. This crowd welcomed me in a way I'd never been welcomed by anybody, and helped me deal with both my body-image issues, and the disaster that was my family.

Capitol wasn't some run-of-the-mill suburban health food place; we sold a hell of a lot more than vitamins and protein bars. We also had fresh-baked goods, and a juice bar, and awesome soups. Dale and Pam, the women who handled all the cooking, became nurturing mother figures, people I could go to after a tough day at school, or if I was having boy problems, or if I just needed a bowl of quality soup. Since my family was disintegrating, it was nice to have them there as a sounding board. Dale was especially patient and listened and encouraged me through those moments of teenage frustration. With a great selection of free food, and a whole bunch of people who listened to and cared for me, going to work was like going home. It was a special place. Plus I was getting paid.

I got a 30 percent discount on all groceries—which was essential, because as noted, Dad wasn't helping us out at all—and though Mom always made sure we had good food around, we took eating healthy to a whole new level. All of our juice came from our Omega-Three juicer, and all of our peanut butter was freshly ground. I was inspired to learn more about my health and my body, and how food affects us, so I spent an inordinate percentage of my salary on nutrition books. I copied recipes either from Dale, or from the cookbooks at the store, and started to cook with more tofu and tempeh. I wanted to be the best athlete I could be and learned that it was crucial to take care of myself both inside and out.

I didn't work a ton of hours or earn a ton of money at

Capitol—sometimes it was as few as twelve hours a month, and the most I'd ever take home for the week was $100—but it was a social and emotional haven, and that was priceless. Customers would come in with cancer and all sorts of ailments that they had alleviated, healed, or managed through herbs and alternative diets, and I started to have gratitude and respect for the miracle that is our bodies.

Capitol also opened my mind on other levels. When I first became a full-time, dedicated athlete, I abstained from *everything*, but now I was a teenager, and when it wasn't track season, I indulged. If I was at a party, and there was beer, I'd drink it. If somebody passed me a joint, I'd take a toke. What with my after-school workouts, and piles of homework, and working at Capitol, I was superhealthy both mentally and physically, so, y'know, why shouldn't I sip a beer or have a little smoke?

But more than that I wanted to be rebellious like everyone else, I wanted to be included, and wanted to be part of the fun. Since kindergarten, I had always felt like I was one of those people on the fringe, and now I was hanging out with the cool kids. And it was good.

My romantic life (if you could call it that) had also become its own form of rebellion. When I was seventeen, I dated a twenty-one-year-old named Shane Osborne—my thinking then was, *Age doesn't matter when you're in love,* but in retrospect, it was kind of creepy—and Mom hated him. She hated the fact that I stayed overnight at his apartment and did who-knows-what, and that he took me into

Manhattan and sneaked me into bars to see ska bands, and that he carted me around on his motorcycle at all hours.

I'll never forget the look on her face when Shane came to pick me up for our first date on that motorcycle. She asked me to have him pick me up in a car next time, but based on her tone, I knew she didn't want him picking me up at all. She clearly disapproved, but I didn't care, because I was thrilled that I had a cool boyfriend. None of the other boys in high school ever took an interest in me, and Shane was sweet and cute, and he made me swoon. There was no way my mom could stop me from seeing him, especially since we both worked together. The more she complained about Shane, the more appealing he became. We had arguments about him all the time, but they always ended in unresolved détente, so I kept enjoying teenage boyfriend bliss.

And seriously, Shane was the coolest boyfriend ever. On my eighteenth birthday, he took me to see an awesome ska double bill of Mighty Mighty Bosstones and the Scofflaws, and I somehow ended up onstage, with the lead singer of the Bosstones serenading me with a funky version of "Happy Birthday." I ended up drinking so much Mount Gay and tonic that on the way back to Long Island, I passed out on the back of Shane's bike. He had to hold onto me with one hand, and steer with the other. It was fabulous.

Sometimes I thought, who needed track? Who needed running? Who needed the Paralympics? Passing out on the back of your twenty-one-year-old boyfriend's motorcycle and smoking with contempo-hippies was what being a teenager was all about. The only things that made me feel good were hanging out with my boyfriend, going to see bands, and drinking. This all ended up being good practice for college.

※

And just like that, high school was over, and things came to a halt. There weren't any more orchestra tours, or international races to prepare for, or after-school club meetings. It was time to go to college, to find my place in the world. I applied to Harvard, Brown, George Washington, Georgetown, and Middlebury, and they all had one thing in common—none were within spitting distance of Long Island. I wanted out. My thinking was, *Screw New York*. Between surgeries, doctors' appointments, and trips to CBGB's, I'd spent enough time in Manhattan for the time being. Plus I figured that I'd end up settling there at some point, and it would be wise to spread my wings and broaden my horizons.

I also kept thinking, *Screw running*. The disappointment of failing at the Paralympics still raged, and whenever I thought about track, I felt defeated. I didn't see much point in going back to running when they might or might not have a women's leg amputee division in the 100m at the next Games. None of the schools I'd applied for had any kind of serious track program, and that's the way I wanted it.

Dad wasn't at all interested in helping with my tuition. How did I know? He flat out said, "I am not paying for college." That blew me away. I'd been a great daughter, and had decent grades, played sports, did all kinds of extracurricular activities, busted my ass to get into a good college, and he was backing out of the deal.

But this wasn't coming entirely from him; the woman he was dating—the very same woman my dad started seeing while he was still living at home—said, "If your kids want to go to some private school, they can pay for it themselves. Aren't any of the New York State schools good enough for them? Sarah's just milking you." When she talked, Dad listened.

Dad even had the balls to tell me, "Carla says there are some really great SUNY schools that have good programs in international affairs." It enraged me that my father was talking about my future with his girlfriend. In less than six months, she'd become significant enough to affect family decisions? Screw that.

I was wait-listed at the Ivy League schools—no surprise, those were my reach schools, anyhow—but I was accepted everywhere else. Ultimately my decision wasn't based on where I wanted to go, but rather where I could afford to go. Middlebury and Georgetown didn't offer me any significant financial aid, and G. W. didn't give me a full ride, but they offered me an academic scholarship with some generous financial aid, so it was off to Washington, D.C. I suspect some fellow students thought I got the package because of my leg, but that was far from the truth. I got good grades, I was involved with a whole lot of extracurricular activities—aside from the Paralympics, we're talking Amnesty International, and Youth Ending Hunger, not to mention the violin studies and orchestra, and the health food store—so on paper, I was a fine all-around student.

I'd socked away about $3,000, which barely made a dent, so I had to take out every student loan imaginable. Mom helped me out with tuition and school expenses as much as she could, but since my father wasn't giving her any money, it was difficult for her, to the point that there were times she wasn't able to pay her heating bill. It was hard enough to be a single mom and take care of two high school teenagers, but stick one of them in a private school, and you're in a hole that's tough to dig out of.

I felt guilty about the whole thing; I mean, hadn't I drained their resources enough with all the trips to the prosthetist's office, and all those medical bills? Maybe I should've gone to a state college to make it easier for all of us. But I refused to let Dad keep me from realizing my college dreams.

Needless to say, I wasn't in the best head space for my first solo sojourn into the world.

⁂

Washington, D.C., was a terrific place to be for a news junkie and idealist such as myself. It felt right to sign up for G. W.'s international affairs program, which would hopefully lead to a job at an embassy or the State Department, someplace I could at once represent the United States, and make a difference in the world.

Yes, I was in a rebellious phase, but I was raised in a Christian household, so "Love thy neighbor as thyself" was instilled into me, whether I liked it or not. So whatever I chose to do with my life, I knew it would involve helping others, and after all those years of racing internationally, I was thinking globally. I liked the idea of working for an international aid organization like the World Health Organization in Geneva, Switzerland, or working in a U.S. Embassy overseas and improving international relations. I didn't go to college to become a hedge fund manager and make a boatload of money; I wanted my life to have a greater purpose in the world, and going to school in the nation's nerve center was the place to learn how to do it.

A few weeks before I headed down to G. W., I called up one of my assigned roommates, Delilah. After exchanging a few pleasantries, Delilah and I sussed out some of the living logistics—which one of us was bringing the coffeemaker, which the microwave, and which the telephone. Then we tried to get to know each other a little bit, chewing over such vital topics as what kind of music we liked, and how we planned to decorate the room, and how much we both liked skiing. I wanted to give and receive as much information as possible, because at that point, the two people I'd be living with for the next nine months were simply Delilah from Cherry Hill, New Jersey, and Donna from Philly, just names on a piece of paper.

One piece of information I didn't discuss with either of the girls: my leg. I didn't know how to bring it up, and I had no idea if they'd ever met an amputee, and I didn't want to freak them out before I even met them. And I also didn't want them changing their minds: What if they called the school and asked to be switched? That would be unbearably humiliating, so I thought it best not to mention it for now.

The closer I got to college, the more nervous I became. I'd been in the same school system since I was five years old, and all the kids knew about the leg, but in a new environment, I'd have to tell the story a hundred times over. I know that people are curious, and I'm happy to explain, but it can get tiresome. Still, I wondered what people would think. Did they have an amputee in their old high school? A friend in a wheelchair? Did it matter if I had a fake leg? Maybe it finally wouldn't.

Immediately after both of my parents and my brother dropped me off at the freshman dorm—yes, Mom and Dad managed to put on a happy face and deliver me to Washington as a unit—things got strange.

Our living area was a two-room suite; one section was a small alcove that had a single twin bed, and the other was somewhat larger, with a pair of twins. Donna arrived first, and she snatched the alcove, and made herself right at home. By the time I showed up, her bed was already made, and her posters were already hung up, including a Matisse print right over the desk. Everything was in its place, and there was a place for everything. (I couldn't be too angry, because I would've probably done more or less the same thing had I gotten there before anybody else, but it was still frustrating.) After she introduced herself, I noticed right away that something was different about her. I didn't want to stare, because I'd had more than my share of being stared at, and I knew how lousy it felt, but I had to figure out what was up. It took me a few minutes of surreptitious glances to realize that her brownish-reddish hair was a wig, and her brownish-reddish eyebrows were drawn on.

Once I realized her hair was fake, my first thought was, *Oh my God, she has cancer.* It wasn't shocking or unfamiliar—I'd seen plenty of cancer kids at various hospitals and athletic events over the years—but it nonetheless gave me pause. I didn't feel comfortable asking her about it—what was I supposed to say, *Ohhhhhhh, when did you get sick? Are you taking radiation? Will you be taking radiation during school?* —and even if I did, I wouldn't know what to say, or how to say it. I'm sure plenty of people feel the same way when they first meet me.

Before we got too deep in conversation, Donna wandered off to the bookstore, and I started to unpack, wondering what Delilah's deal was. Ten minutes later, after answering an insistent knock at the door, I found out.

I stared at Delilah for a few seconds, then said, "I know you!"

She said, "You do?"

"We met at Paddy's ski camp!"

Delilah peered at me. "Holy shit," she said. "You're right."

Turned out that Delilah and I had met two years before on one of Paddy Rossbach's ski outings, and we bonded there primarily because we were the only sixteen-year-olds on the trip. We didn't become best friends, but she felt comfortable enough with me that a couple of days after we met, she pulled me aside and told me, "I got my period. I can't believe I'm going to have to ski with a pad on."

I asked her, "Why don't you use a tampon?"

She said, "I've never used a tampon. How does it work?"

I thought, *Duh,* said, "Get with it, Delilah," then taught the poor girl how to use a tampon. And yet she didn't want to stay in touch with me. Go figure.

It wasn't a surprise that we didn't recognize each other from our conversations. At the ski camp, neither of us knew the other one's last name—she was just Delilah from Jersey, and I was just Sarah from New York—and on the phone, neither of us said anything about our disabilities.

After we caught up for a few minutes, it dawned on us that our room was a miniature rehab ward: two amputees and a cancer patient. I said to Delilah, "Wait a minute. We're supposed to believe that this was random? That all the freshman names were put in a computer, and it randomly put the three disabled girls in the class in the same room? This isn't a coincidence."

She was pretty nonplussed, as was Donna. We kicked it around for a while and decided that maybe it was coming from a good place, maybe the administration wanted us to have a built-in support system for each other, and maybe they thought since we were all missing something—in my and Delilah's case, legs, and in Donna's, hair—we could help each other make it through our freshman year. (In theory, that wasn't a terrible idea, but look at what happened during fire drills: You've got Delilah strapping on her two prosthetics, me jamming on mine, and Donna in the bathroom drawing on eyebrows and fixing her wig. It would've been nice to have a fully abled body around in the event of an actual fire.)

The fact of the matter is, it was insulting. If there were only, say, ten African-American kids in the class, and they put three of them in the same room, the NAACP wouldn't be too thrilled. It would be straight-up racist, and nobody could possibly deny that. So from that perspective, we were like African-Americans, circa Jim Crow. Delilah, Donna, and I were being segregated and ghettoized. Did the school put all the Asians in one room, and all the Hispanics in another? All my other friends' rooms seemed to be mixed, why wasn't ours?

Admittedly, part of the reason I wanted to switch rooms was that Donna went a bit off the rails—she stole some of our clothes, money often went missing, and she called our boyfriends behind our backs—and neither Delilah nor I were comfortable living with her. But mostly, it was the principle of the thing.

It was an ugly situation, so me being me, I called the school on it. I mentioned my theory to my resident advisor, and he said I'd need to speak to somebody above him. Delilah and I did finally get a meeting with the proper person, and it got us nowhere. He stonewalled us, telling us time and again that the Disability Ghetto wasn't purposeful, claiming that all freshman student rooms were assigned strictly by lottery system. The school's position was that it indeed was just a random coincidence, which dumbfounded me.

I said, "Random? Really? Well, with odds like that we should go buy a lottery ticket because that seems pretty lucky. I'm sure there's a journalist out there who might want to know about how G. W. treats its disabled students. They slap them in one room on the third floor, like they're lepers!" That was an empty threat, because between classes and homework, I didn't really have the time or energy to launch a media campaign.

On the plus side, when Donna moved out the following semester, the university never forced another roommate on us. I think they wanted to keep us quiet. You take your victories where you can get them.

And then, out of nowhere, I started to miss running. Sports had always made me feel good about my body, and I was a bit lost without it. There were no running tracks near GWU, and I didn't have a nice even oval to run on, so I had to hit the streets. It wasn't ideal, but it was a great release nonetheless.

That year I competed in the 1994 U.S. Disabled Track & Field Championships, because the Atlanta Paralympics were coming up in 1996, and I wanted to keep the door open, and gauge my fitness and skill level. Plus the Nationals were in Baltimore, which was just up the road from GWU. (Truth be told, I probably wouldn't have gone if the meet hadn't been so close.)

I invited Delilah to come and hang out, and she initially said no, which I understood, because she wasn't an athlete—she'd been the batgirl on her high school softball team but had never played much of anything. But the more she thought about it, the more intrigued she became. Her parents weren't proactive in terms of getting her involved in athletics, and she never had a guy like David Balsley to show her that almost anything is possible, so the fact that I was getting out in the world and *participating* was revolutionary for her.

While my parents spent years traveling to and from track meets in the chase for my Paralympic dreams, Delilah's working-class parents didn't even want to talk about the fact that she was missing her legs, let alone empower her to run on prosthetics. I had a huge support system, and poor Delilah had never even heard of the Paralympics.

Considering all that, it wasn't a surprise that Delilah chose to keep her disability literally under wraps, opting for long skirts and pants over shorts and short dresses. I can't imagine how many times Delilah had somebody wander up to her and say, "Oh my God, your roommate is so amazing, what with her one leg," without knowing she was missing *both* of her legs. That had to be frustrating for her, but it was her choice. She'd made the decision to hide her disability, and that's the way she always had been; she even had a high school teacher who didn't know she was an amputee until she wrote an essay about it at the end of the semester.

Delilah also had a rough childhood. Her father was an angry man, and not totally enlightened, and I think he was more comfortable with her prosthetics all hidden away. Delilah wanted to look like a normal girl, but her father demanded it. As messed up as my family was, they were wonderful in how they dealt with my leg. Delilah's, not so much. My family never made me feel ashamed. Her family was . . . different.

But that didn't stop her from taking up running. And you know what? She was pretty damn good.

Despite our differing attitude toward our respective disabilities, we got along famously, and chose to room together again in our sophomore year. One of the many reasons I wanted to stick with her was because when it came to dating, Delilah was a great sounding board. I could talk to her about things I couldn't discuss with other girlfriends, because she, like no one else I'd ever met, knew *exactly* what I was going through with my leg. She understood what it was like to be uncertain about your body, about how and when to reveal yourself. All of the girls in my circle had the same insecurities about boys, but they'd never *get it* like Delilah would. How could they? They had two working legs. Delilah didn't. I was lucky to have a soul sister right across the room.

In 1995, Delilah came with me to the U.S. Disabled Track & Field Championships at MIT in Boston. It was her first competition, so I showed her the ropes, and introduced her to all the other athletes I'd trained and raced with, to my sponsors at Flex-Foot, and to the U.S. team prosthetist. It was a great scene trackside at MIT that year; the field was flush with talent vying for a spot on the 1996 Paralympic Team, and there was a palpable buzz in the air.

Delilah didn't have any running legs yet, so she had to race in her walking legs. She had been dealing with some sores on her stumps, but she toughed it out, and when the gun went off, so did Delilah. She ran an impressive race, and I realized that this girl was a tough competitor. That one race changed her life, and I was proud to have had a hand in it.

Interestingly enough, after the meet, she started wearing shorts in public. Every time I saw her walking around Washington, head held high, prosthetics out there for the world to see, I smiled. I guess I was rubbing off on her. I didn't know just how much until much later.

※

I met Alex halfway through my freshman year. He was half-Mormon, half-Jewish, raised in a commune in Utah, then moved to St. Lucia, where his hippie parents became scuba instructors. He was a skinny guy, fit from lots of rock climbing and wind surfing. He had long hair he liked to pull back in a ponytail, soft brown eyes, and the sweetest smile. He was interested in environmental studies, and he always seemed up for an adventure, anything from a hike in Virginia, to hitting the bars with our new fake IDs.

Alex was a stellar boyfriend, and we had a wonderful, loving relationship. He was so sweet and tender with me, and I melted with every kiss. This was the first time I was ever 100 percent comfortable being naked in front of a guy, without my prosthetic. I never worried about much of anything when we were together. Whenever he took me in his arms, my fractured family on Long Island felt a million miles away. I fell, and I fell hard.

Come sophomore year, our relationship changed. Who knows why? We were kids, and when you're kids, sometimes things just happen. Halfway through the first semester we broke up. The following week, Dad called: He was getting remarried, and he wanted me to come to the wedding.

It was a one-two punch to the gut. Dumped by my first true love, then asked by the man who dumped my mother to celebrate his new life? Give me a break. Dad was replacing us with another family, a younger wife, and younger kids, and I'm supposed to raise a glass to that? Hell, no.

In the midst of all this turmoil, it was little surprise my grades started to slip. It was also little surprise I dated a blow-off trust fund party boy whose favorite thing to do in the world was get wrecked. It was also little surprise that I became entirely disillusioned with the Washington-white-guy-bullshit political games. It was also little surprise that I blew off class after class after class. It was also little surprise that I regularly partied hard and drank to the point of blacking out.

It was also little surprise that I lost all touch with reality.

I slept all day and stayed up all night, and closed the Georgetown bars, and drank tons of beer at the Sigma Chi house, and watched music videos into the wee hours of the morning. I stopped caring about pretty much everything, and my joy for life all but faded away. The downward spiral kept picking up momentum, and when I failed one of my midterms—the first test I'd ever failed in my life—I decided to seek out some help.

After a bit of research, I found a therapist that took my insurance, no easy task in Washington, D.C. She listened closely to my myriad problems, and at the end of the session, suggested that I start taking Prozac.

My initial thought was *I don't want to take this stuff*, but three seconds later, I admitted that I had to do *something*. I needed to get my life and my head together—drinking until I blacked out, and living like a vampire, and not showering regularly, and never leaving the house wasn't working—so in the summer of 1995, with my grades in the toilet, and my brain who-knows-where, I took a medical leave of absence from George Washington, and moved back to Long Island for a semester.

When I returned home, I felt like a big loser, a complete failure. I was this shining star of an athlete and student, and only two years after leaving New York, I completely cracked under the pressure, losing my head, in all senses of the phrase. Fortunately, my mother was a pillar of support, and was happy to help nurse me back to mental health. I regularly visited a therapist, who helped me to deal with all the Reinertsen stuff that I hadn't ever gotten a handle on. I stabilized and normalized, reconnected with my family and the world. The depression lifted incrementally, but at least I was moving in a positive direction.

I landed a job at a telecommunications company called CT Networks. The position, sales team assistant, was a snooze—the highlights of my day were data entry and collating training manuals—but it was tangible office experience I could put on my resume, plus I needed to make money, so I was grateful to have the gig. I also enrolled in some classes at Nassau Community College, and it took me a grand total of one week to realize I had to get the hell out of there. Nobody studied, and nobody cared. The most competitive outlet the students had was the parking lot; if you got a good spot, you won. It made me appreciate the classes and facilities we had at George Washington University. I missed G. W. and resolved to get my degree, as soon as possible.

That said, Nassau wasn't a *complete* waste of time. I took a TV production class, which I adored, and it afforded me the opportunity to produce a television broadcast in their on-campus studio. For the final exam, I put together a video on disabled sports and the history of the Paralympics, and it was a rush to be in the control booth with all those monitors, picking the camera shots for the live interviews and pre-taped segments. *Who knows,* I thought, *this could lead to something.*

I wanted to return to G. W., but I also thought it might be healthy for me to get out of the country. The Atlanta Paralympics were just around the corner, and I was conflicted: *Can I do this? Do I want to go through the entire training regimen? Will I end up getting screwed and running against arm amputees again?* I didn't even bother trying to find out. With all the disappointments of my life—my family, Barcelona, depression—I couldn't bring myself to do it. I didn't even go to Nationals.

But in January, I did go back to Spain.

G. W. offered a study abroad program at a small private university called Universidad Nebrissensis. Because it was a G. W. program, any credits I earned would transfer and count toward my graduation requirements, and since I was already playing catch-up, it was critical that I could use every credit I earned abroad. Being across the Atlantic would also allow me the chance to ease my way back into the college and assert my independence.

As was the case when I went to the Paralympics, I fell in love with Spain. Madrid was such a vibrant and lively place, and I wanted to take advantage of all that the city had to offer. The combination of living alone in a strange country and perfecting my Spanish made me feel like I could conquer the world again. I worked hard, and did well in my classes, but also had a hell of a lot of fun. There was so much to explore and see in this new city: the Thiessen museum, the Greco paintings at the Prado, Retiro Park, and the Palacio. I snacked on tapas at the cervezerias, sipped hot chocolate, and ate churros after long nights of dancing at the clubs. My new friends and I lived it up, and frankly, I deserved it.

That April, I was at a club in Madrid, dancing my ass off, and I bumped into a friend from G. W. After a minute or three of *Oh My God I Can't Believe You're Here,* she filled me in on what Delilah was up to, and after I got the whole scoop, it felt like somebody had kicked me in the gut.

As far as I knew, Delilah and I were still tight—while I was still decompressing in Long Island, we had one awesome weekend down in D.C.; she took me out to dinner, and an amazing Henry Rollins spoken word performance—but it was strange that during that entire weekend, she never once mentioned she'd transferred to Georgetown.

Nor did she mention she had started running track at her new school.

Nor did she mention she'd gotten prosthetic racing legs almost identical to mine.

Nor did she mention she'd decided to train for the 1996 Paralympic Games.

I was shocked. I'd introduced her to the world of track and field, and she couldn't even tell me she'd dived in.

My initial thoughts: Why was my alleged best friend being sneaky about this? Is it because she wants to copy my life? Does she want to become me? It was all very strange, very *Single White Female.* We'd lived together for two years and I had grown to love her like a sister, and I thought she felt the same way about me. Apparently I was sadly mistaken, because true sisters tell each other everything, and Delilah didn't tell me a damn thing.

I wanted to give Delilah a ring, but I knew it would be a long conversation, and I couldn't afford a long transatlantic phone call; besides, this was an in-person discussion. I couldn't write a letter, because I wanted my communication with her to be two ways, not one-sided. I wanted to hear Delilah's version of the story, but it would have to wait until I returned to the United States the next month.

When I got home, I had a more pressing matter, so my first stop was Mike Joyce's Leg Shack. I was having problems with my prosthetic leg—it's possible I put on a bit of weight, what with all the fiestas and siestas—and some size adjustments were a top priority.

After I sat down in the examination room, Mike shut the door, shook my hand, and said, "Sarah, it's so good to see you. I've been wanting to talk to you for a while. How're you doing?" His tone was serious to the point of somberness.

I said, "Um, great, I suppose." I filled him in on Spain, but didn't mention anything about the meltdown that sent me there in the first place.

He said, "Seriously. How're you doing?"

I said, "Seriously. I'm great."

He shook his head. "I've been hearing a lot of things about you."

"Like what?"

He took a deep breath and asked, "Do you have a drug problem?"

"What?!"

"There're a lot of rumors going around about what you've been going through. People are saying you're an alcoholic and a drug addict."

"What people?" Who would say something like that about me? And to Mike Joyce.

"Somebody from the U.S. track team."

I did some quick math. The only person on the track team who knew about the meltdown was Delilah. My guess: She mentioned it to somebody, who told somebody else, who told Mike.

So not only did Delilah lie to me about her transfer to Georgetown, and about her track and field goals, but she also talked smack about me to people I'd known since I was twelve, and I was outraged. I didn't think she was telling them about my partying days at school out of concern, or to get me help; it seemed like she was more interested in ruining my reputation.

This had to be dealt with.

The next day, I called her up at her apartment in Washington, D.C. After some superficial catch-up conversation, I said, "So, Delilah, I heard some weird rumors about me from somebody on the track team. Did you hear anything?"

She said, "No. No. No, I didn't." And even tried to reassure me that had she heard anything about me at the track meet, she would have defended me.

And just like that, I started to cry, because I knew she was lying. This woman whom I lived with for two years, whom I grew from teenager to young woman with, whom I thought was my soul sister, broke my heart.

I couldn't get under control, so I said, "I've got to go," and then I hung up.

I never called her back. I tried not to dwell on it. But I couldn't let it go. Hadn't we always encouraged each other, and now she was going to lie to my face and push me out in the process? I had never had a friend betray me like that and I was stunned by Delilah's audacity, especially since she knew what led to my downward spiral. Did it make her feel better to tarnish my reputation? Never before or since had I seen worse sportsmanship.

Delilah made the 1996 U.S. Paralympic Team in the 100m dash. Her opponents: arm amputees. As was the case in 1992, there weren't enough women to fill out an entire field, so Delilah also failed to earn a medal at the games. It wasn't much different from my Paralympic race, and I was relieved that I didn't enter, because it would've been '92 all over again.

Although I didn't participate, I went down to Atlanta to watch the games, because the Amputee Coalition of

America was holding their annual meeting, and Flex-Foot, my sponsor who had been giving me feet since 1992, flew me in to take part in a Team Flex-Foot autograph signing. And who's sitting next to me at the event? Good old Delilah. My one-time soul sister.

After we finished signing poster after poster after poster, I asked Delilah to come out to the lobby with me. I said, "Okay, apparently a lot of people have been talking about me, and what I've been going through, and I don't know how the word got around, but it's all pointing back to you. You're the only person who knows all this intimate stuff about me from school. These are people who've seen me grow up from a twelve-year-old pipsqueak to a twenty-one-year-old woman. These are my people, and if somebody said something to them about me, do you honestly think they're not going to tell me?"

She lost it. "You don't know how hard it was to see you getting all that attention. You don't know what it was like. You're the one on all the posters and all everybody on the team and at Flex-Foot talks about is you, you, you, Sarah, Sarah, Sarah."

I said, "Delilah, I've been running since I was twelve! You expect them to forget about me? I've been doing this for years. You just started running a year ago. You'll be on the posters when they use the photos from this year's games."

Delilah continued to attack, and the longer we argued, the stiffer and colder she became. She never apologized, never acknowledged that she'd done anything wrong, and

I was stunned by her lack of integrity and ownership. The fact that she showed no emotion or remorse got me bawling, right there in the hotel lobby.

And then one of the guys on the team called, "Come on, Delilah. The bus is going back to the Paralympic Village. We got to roll."

Delilah looked at me, shrugged, and said, "Okay. I've gotta go."

And she went. That was the last time I had any meaningful conversation with her.

As the games went on, it was confirmed by my friends on the team that yes, it was Delilah who'd dished the dirt—and the dishing was indeed dirty, not coming from a place of friendship and concern. Surely if her motives had been altruistic she would have also talked to my Mom, or checked in and made sure I was getting help. It was shit-talking, pure and simple. She fell into a spiral of jealousy, and she wanted to cut me down. It was pathetic.

I went into damage control mode, but it turned out there wasn't all that much damage that needed controlling. Most everybody in the running circle was unbelievably sympathetic, because they *knew*. They *knew* about my parents' divorce. They *knew* about how Barcelona killed me. They *knew* why I wasn't competing. And they cared.

Delilah only ran for one more year after that, and then gave up the sport altogether. For the next several years, she claimed she was the first female amputee to ever run NCAA track, which was technically true, as she did run for one year at Georgetown to prepare for the Paralympics, but it seemed a bit misleading to pitch it like she was this historic and pioneering figure in sports for women with disabilities. The fact of the matter is, she was just following in my footsteps, just like I had followed in the footsteps of other amputee runners before me. Delilah raced for only two or three years, which is commendable, but doesn't amount to much in the disabled athletics big picture. Worst of all, she did little to get more disabled women involved in sport, choosing instead to focus on a career in modeling and acting.

As far as I was concerned, Delilah blew it on every level imaginable, and frankly, I was glad she was out of my life.

One week after I returned home from Spain, my uncle David was found dead from a cocaine overdose. He was discovered in a hotel room by a maid, and he'd already been dead for several days. As far as anybody could figure, his drug buddies ripped him off—he had no money on him, no ID, no nothing—and the only reason he was identified was because he had a recent parking ticket in his pocket. He died in the company of a bunch of party-boy losers who didn't give a damn about him. I mean, they took his wallet. How cold do you have to be to steal from a dead man?

That was a big wake-up call for me. I'd spent a lot of time at G. W. experimenting—the club scene, the partying, the booze—but it never dawned on me that experimentation could lead to suicide. Yes, I mean suicide, because the way I looked at it, my uncle killed himself. It may not have been premeditated, but his destructive choices led to his tragic death, the key word here being "choices." I didn't want to die; I had just come back from living in Europe where I saw just how much more there was to see and do in the world. It was time to start living well, to take care of myself again. It was a call to action and I wasn't going to waste my life anymore.

I was totally burnt out and disillusioned with the competitive track and field world—not being able to run in an even field time and again will do that to you—but I still loved running, still loved being labeled as a runner. With Paddy Rossbach and her marathons in the back of my head, I figured it was time to give distance running a shot.

Mom and I signed up for a 5K race, which was a big deal for me, because at that point, the longest I'd ever run was half a mile. I bought issue after issue of *Runner's World* magazine, and snipped out all the articles I could find about preparing for a 5K. Mom worked with me, and David and Paddy gave me all kinds of advice, and the entire process was supportive, warm, and fuzzy.

The race was near our house on Long Island. It was July 4th, a warm sunny summer morning, and it was exciting and fresh to be at another starting line. I was nervous, but there wasn't the same pressure I knew from the track, because I was only one of five hundred racers, most of whom were running just for the sake of running. It was about fun. My only competition was myself.

We didn't run for the entire race, because, well, I couldn't. We walked up the hills, and jogged slowly on the flats, and slowed down at all the water stops, and forty-five minutes later, I finished my first 5K. I liked the challenge of distance running, or in my case run/walking. The best part about the whole thing was that there were runners and walkers of all levels, so I wasn't the last one to cross the finish line, so that was a victory all its own. I knew how *fast* I could go, and now it was time to find out how *far* I could go.

When I went back to G. W. that fall, my depression had all but washed away, and I was 89 percent clean and sober—I was in college, remember, and that 11 percent of indulging is part of the deal—and I entered the Georgetown Classic 10K. I didn't want to run it alone, so I dragged along my friends M.G. and Damon, who were more than happy to join me after I told them there would be free beer at the finish line. Again, I finished, and again, I wasn't the last person to cross the finish line, and again, my confidence level soared.

In 1997, my senior year, I again went to the U.S. Disabled Track Championships in Springfield, Massachusetts, not as a sprinter, but as a distance runner. I was the only woman to sign up for the 5,000m, so I had to run with the men. That didn't faze me a bit; actually, I was psyched to see how I measured up to the boys.

The night before the race, I couldn't sleep thanks to some heinous gas pains. Everything was clogged up—I was having serious digestive issues. I threw down Gas-X pill after Maalox pill, and nothing. I tossed and turned all night, and made countless trips to the toilet in hopes something would happen to make the pain go away. I didn't sleep a wink, and when the alarm went off, my stomach still felt wretched, and I didn't know if I could do the race.

But I went for it. This was the national Championships, it's only once a year, so just do it. That was my attitude, but I'm still not sure if it was the best idea.

It was a ninety-five-degree day, and being that we were on a track, there wasn't a patch of shade to be found. But when the starter's pistol went off, the weather and the stomachache didn't matter. I had no choice but to run. What with the heat and the abdominal throbbing, I felt like I was going to collapse, but I refused to stop pumping my legs. I just focused on the track lanes directly ahead of me, one step at a time. And then, with six laps to go, just when I thought I was going to burst . . . I did.

I was wearing navy shorts, and after I pissed myself, I was mildly relieved that I'd worn my white shorts the day before for the short distance races. I knew they were wet, but I didn't dare slow down or look down. And I was afraid to stop running. I told myself, *Finish the race, nobody's going to care if you pissed your shorts, just finish the race. Grete Waitz finished the New York City Marathon in 1988, and she had diarrhea. This is nothing. At least you aren't shitting yourself.*

And this race is a lot shorter than a marathon. Be strong like Grete.

I crossed the finish line ahead of one of the male competitors, which made me smile despite the condition of my shorts. I could barely stand up straight, let alone walk, so, bent over and clutching at my stomach, I hobbled to the medical tent.

The medical staff took my vitals and said I should probably visit the nearest hospital, but if my mother and I insisted on driving back to New York, that would be fine, as long as I *immediately* went to a doctor. Mom calmly but quickly drove back to NYC, and three hours later, I was in the hospital. The doctor said my primary symptoms weren't gas, but rather a urinary tract infection, which, thanks to the hard run, had morphed into a full-blown kidney infection. I had a 104-degree temperature and was severely dehydrated, so they hooked me up to an IV to get the antibiotics into my system as quickly as possible. Talk about a crazy day.

That was my first official competitive long distance race. It wasn't an auspicious start, so naturally, I wanted more.

CHAPTER 4

JUMP AT THE CHANCE

For most who've dabbled in running, there's a certain mystique about a marathon. It's a holy grail of sorts, a seemingly unattainable goal, the race that modern runners have been measured by since 1921, the year the twenty-six miles and 385 yards distance was standardized.

The New York City Marathon is acknowledged to be one of the coolest in the world, right up there with the Boston Marathon and the Olympics. The route goes through all five boroughs and takes the racers past streets and landmarks that all New Yorkers are intimately familiar with. I've driven over the Verrazano Bridge zillions of times, but seeing all the racers sprint, run, and jog over the bridge, with their multicolored track gear—it's the helicopter shot of the twenty-thousand-plus runners taking up every lane on every level of that bridge that always gets me—is quite a sight. The finish line is also an emotional moment; to see the reaction as they cross the tape is at once moving and inspiring. Each year a different drama unfolds: agony and heartache, joy and triumph.

The race is covered on live television in the New York metro area, and in our house it was a tradition to tune in. We'd zip home from church on marathon Sunday (which is generally the first Sunday in November) so we could watch the entire event from start to finish. We didn't want to miss one second of my hero Grete Waitz, that elegant and strong Norwegian woman who ran through the streets of New York at an unfathomable pace. I wanted to be like Grete. Knowing that Paddy Rossbach had completed nine marathons helped make the concept more than a pipe dream, and falling in love with long distance running turned the dream into a goal.

There's a meditative quality about distance running that, once my body got used to the punishment of the road, I grew to love, so much so that 5Ks and 10Ks felt like appetizers. I was ready for a full twenty-six-mile meal, so I signed up to run the 1997 NYC Marathon. The longest distance I'd run to that point was seventeen miles, and that wasn't even consecutive miles, but rather seventeen miles in a twenty-four-hour period. But I figured if I could do seventeen miles in twenty-four hours, twenty-six-plus miles in six-plus hours wasn't unrealistic. I also knew I had years of experience hiking through the woods with my family during our summer vacations in Highland Lake, New York, and if I could wander over bumpy terrain for hours, I could hike through semi-bumpy Manhattan. Sure, I wanted to run the marathon like Grete, but one step at a time; at the very least I could hike or walk my way to the finish line.

The entry process was a relative breeze; most runners have to enter a lottery to win a slot in the field, but the

New York Road Runners Club has a tradition of being incredibly supportive of disabled athletes, so after applying for one of the Achilles slots in the race, I was given an entry form for the NYC Marathon, even though the race was three months away. I filled out the race form and sent it along with my $65 check, and when the mailbox shut, in that moment, I was both terrified and exhilarated. No turning back. It was real.

I went straight home and immediately called David Balsley, because if anybody could get me through twenty-six miles, it was him. We discussed a tentative schedule, and I mentioned to him that I'd clipped some marathon training plans from *Runner's World,* but David told me I'd need a completely different approach. "Look Sarah, you can't run fast enough to cover all the mileage those plans suggest right now. You're an amputee runner, and you have to train differently, and your focus should be on *time.*"

"Time? I just want to finish the damn race."

"I mean, the amount of time you'll be spending on your prosthetic. You have to get comfortable being on it nonstop for hours at a time." That's something I'd never considered, but it made total sense. "So when you make your little schedule, instead of you saying, 'I'm running ten miles on Saturday,' I want you to say, 'I'm doing a three hour jog/walk on Saturday.' I don't care how much you run, or how much you walk, although I'd love for you to run as much as possible. I just want you to do the full three hours without stopping. The Saturday after, three-and-a-half hours. The

Saturday after, four. Then four-and-a-half, then five, and so on, up until race day."

"Sounds good." I paused, then asked, "Will you run the race with me?"

I knew he wouldn't have a chance to train for the race, but considering everything he's done as an ultra-marathon runner, David could roll out of bed tomorrow morning and run a marathon without breaking a sweat. He said, "You bet, no problem." Once training started, it was just like the old days, but on the other hand, it was an entirely new adventure and I felt that athletic spark again.

My friends had all graduated in May, and my social life was all but nonexistent, so I was happy to spend five days a week and a huge chunk of my weekends running. Plus training was therapeutic, and it helped me make smarter choices; I wasn't drinking or staying out late, and I was cooking and eating healthier foods; homemade whole grain muffins and fruit smoothies replaced pizza and beer. I even pulled out all those old cookbooks and health books from Capitol Health and became a vegan.

Given that I had practically zero free time, I had to multitask at every given opportunity. On my Saturday runs, I'd throw on my Sony Walkman—Discmans were too sensitive to run with, and this was well before iPods—and then jog/walk six miles to the Whole Foods in Georgetown with an empty backpack strapped onto my shoulders. First I'd get some water to rehydrate, then do my shopping, slide on my now-food-filled backpack, and hoof it home the six miles back as quickly as I could. That's not the kind of thing they'd necessarily suggest in *Runner's World* . . . but maybe they should.

Every longish walk was an opportunity to train, and when my classmates saw me jog/walking from place to place, they thought I was nuts. I was taking seventeen credits worth of classes at G. W. (eighteen is considered a full load), so between that, prepping for the race for ten hours a week, taking a pair of hard-core yoga classes, and doing grunt work as a minimum wage slave at a media consulting firm, I was pretty maxed out, and everybody knew it—except, of course, for me.

I didn't go out much, and I didn't miss the bars or the party scene one bit. I went to bed early so I could go on long training runs through the best of Washington, D.C., past the Jefferson Memorial with a bonus stair climb up to the Lincoln Memorial, then down to the Capitol building, and past the White House, then back to my studio apartment in Foggy Bottom. With each run, I became both physically and emotionally stronger. I was back on track, and jog/walking toward a bright future.

※

In terms of how I'd perform at the marathon, I had no expectations. How could I? My longest training jog/walk lasted five-and-a-half hours, which had completely wiped me out; I was so sore the next day that I couldn't even muster the energy to walk to the library.

Now that I knew I could jog/walk for over five-plus hours, I could start crunching some numbers: How many miles did I cover on that five-hour training session? How fast was I running? Okay, let's say I did three miles per hour, multiply that times five, and we're talking fifteen miles, but the question is how much slower would I be for the last eleven miles? Or can I even make those eleven miles? I eventually guesstimated that I could do it in seven hours . . . or possibly eight . . . or maybe nine. Truth is, my time didn't matter. I was going to finish, dammit, even if I had to walk twenty of the twenty-six miles.

And then, in a blink, it was November 1, the day before the race.

I crashed at David's apartment on the Upper East Side. He and his beautiful wife, Maggie, welcomed me in, but I was dazed, not believing that I was actually going to do a marathon. Dave tried to reassure me and showed me to their guest bedroom. The city was alive and loud: Ambulances and trucks roared by, and people yelled at one another, but the noise in my head drowned out everything. I began to doubt myself and question the wisdom of signing up for this ridiculous race in the first place. But there was no backing out. Too many people were rooting for me, and I couldn't let them down. Hell, I couldn't let *me* down.

At 4:00 a.m., after a grand total of three hours of nervous sleep, we took a car service to the starting area, arriving just before the Verrazano closed for the day. In the spirit of helping out disabled runners, the NYC Marathon organizers set up an early start time for those of us who thought we'd take more than seven hours to finish; we could start at 8:30, while the other racers began at 10:45. At one point, I thought that I might be able to get in under seven, but I remembered seeing twenty thousand marathoners cross the Verrazano on television, and it dawned on me that I could be slower just trying to negotiate my way along with that huge pack of runners.

A Sunday *New York Times* in tow, we found a tiny spot on the wet lawn in what's called the Start Village and tried to relax; it was a cold brisk morning so we were bundled in sweatshirts and sweatpants. And I wound up not really reading the newspaper, but rather sitting on it to make the ground a bit warmer since we still had a couple hours to wait. I distracted myself by listening to the dozens of racers from other countries speaking to each other in their native languages. It was a veritable United Nations of runners, with the athletes wearing the colors of their nations' flags; some even carried flags, or pinned them to the back of their jerseys.

The Start Village is a quarter-mile away from the starting line, so at 8:00 a.m., we headed over to the bridge. About 150 early starting runners gathered around: a few blind athletes with their guides; a handful of folks in wheelchairs; some elderly people with walkers, and, of course, a certain short blonde chick from Long Island with a missing leg.

The New York City Marathon isn't kicked off with a mere starter's pistol—that would be far too small for the

Big Apple. No, the New York City Marathon is launched with a cannon . . . or at least it is for the regular runners. For us early starters, it's "On your mark, get set, go," and then a little foghorn. Not exactly what you'd call glamorous, but it sounded grand to me.

I knew I wouldn't be able to maintain a standard leg-over-leg gait for the entire race, so I eased into the race with a hop/skip step, which didn't put as much strain on my lower left back and helped me to conserve my energy. (They say the longest journey starts with a single step, not a single hop/skip, but you have to work with what you've got.) So David slowly jogged next to me as I hop/skipped my way across the bridge toward the NYC skyline, and the long day had officially begun.

❈

I had taken a public relations course earlier that year at George Washington, and I'd become pretty media-savvy, so a month before the race, I faxed out press releases to a bunch of New York and national television and print outlets, saying, "Paralympic athlete, 100m world record holder, and New York native Sarah Reinertsen is doing her first marathon, blah blah blah." As a struggling college student who didn't have any shoe or clothing sponsors, buying multiple pairs of Nike Airs had become a hardship, so I figured some TV coverage could lead to some sorely needed sponsorships. The plan worked: A couple newspapers interviewed me, and the NBC affiliate tracked me down and told me to look for their crew when we hit Brooklyn, around the ten-mile mark.

I was in pretty good shape as we continued running toward the Queensborough Bridge—we'd already been on the course for about three hours, and, thanks to David's regimen, I could do three hours in my sleep—so my chipper banter with the interviewer and the ear-to-ear grin they showed on the 11:00 news that night were completely sincere and legit. I was having a great time, and everybody told me it showed. Len Berman, the NBC sports anchor back in the studio, even signed off the piece with a little, "Way to go, Sarah! Represent New York!" I felt like a true hometown hero.

Almost immediately after the interview, the elite runners started blowing by us, which was incredible. We had the best view imaginable of those Kenyan wunderkinds effortlessly breezing through their five-minute miles. Then came the TV trucks, then came the average Joes who, what with their 2:30 finish times, really weren't that average.

The crowds along the streets of New York were magical, and by the time we ran up First Avenue in Manhattan, I actually felt like Grete Waitz. Unfortunately when I reached the water stop at the sixteenth mile, my lower back started to really bother me; I took a moment to eat a Clif Bar and take a couple Advil. The ibuprofen didn't seem to do much, so we stopped at the next medical tent a few miles later, and had them rub some Ben-Gay onto my lower left back. The smelly gel worked wonders, and the weird tingling heat kept me loose enough to get me through the next couple miles.

An hour later, at mile twenty, my back started singing again, but I didn't really notice, because my entire body was a bundle of pain, not to mention that I had nothing left in my tank. Just like a lot of first-time marathoners, I hit the wall, but David wouldn't let that stop me: "C'mon, Sarah," he yelled, "you can do this. We've only got a 10K to go, that's just six miles, you can cover that no problem. Just don't stop moving; it's going to be harder to start up again if you quit." He chuckled a little, then continued, "You're a tough chick, not just some blonde bimbo. You can finish this silly race!" I laughed, then soon fell into an auto-pilot zone where I was in almost a comatose state, which might've been my body's way of helping me compartmentalize my exhaustion and pain. (I once heard former championship cyclist and television commentator Phil Liggett say about the Tour de France, "You have to learn how to put up with a certain amount of suffering." Even though he was talking about bicycle riding, you can certainly apply the sentiment to marathons. When your legs beg you to stop, you ignore their protests and keep pushing forward regardless.) Fortunately the onlookers woke me up, which is why I love big city races; the crowd support is always amazing. Their encouraging shouts and nonstop applause have carried many a runner across many a finish line.

And then came the rains. (It was in the forecast, and I was mentally prepared for it, but it still sucked.) And we're not talking a drizzle, or even a steady November shower. We're talking torrential downpours, accompanied by twenty-some-odd mile per hour winds. My clothes and shoes got drenched, and the moisture added what felt like ten pounds to my weight. I kept thinking, *What's going to happen to my prosthetic? Is it going to rust? Do I have any WD-40 at home?*

I started to complain about the rain, and Dave said, "So what? It's rain. Big deal. You gonna melt?" And then, to cheer me up and distract me, he started doing imitations of all the good cheers we had gotten along the course today. He did the guy that shouted out, "Hey all right, baby, the Bronx loves ya! You're gonna make it sweetheart," and the animated lady in Harlem who screamed, "Ohmigod, you are unbelievable! You go, girlfriend! You go!" That local flavor is part of what makes New York runs so magical.

And then, arm thrust in the air and a grin plastered onto my face, I crossed the finish line in 6:32. This was just as cool as an Olympic medal, and it was even more satisfying than breaking the 100m world record, because it was *sooooo* much more difficult.

After the race, with the rain still turning Manhattan into a flood zone, we walked back to David's apartment on the Upper East Side—and that's right, we *walked,* because it's impossible to find a cab in New York on Marathon Day. My family was waiting for me at Dave's place; Mom, her boyfriend (now husband) Pete Fuentes, and my Aunt Simone, gave me hugs and kisses. We ordered some Chinese, and

I shoved down dinner, then headed off to LaGuardia Airport, because I had to catch the last shuttle back to D.C., so I'd be able to make classes the next morning. I wore my medal on the plane like a big old dork and basked in the glow of my victory.

The victory, however, was short-lived.

The next morning I learned that if you take the early 8:30 race start, and you finish in under seven hours, you're disqualified, because they don't want the masses taking unfair advantage of the jump on the crowd. So technically, I had disqualified myself by completing the race in under seven hours. It was a small bummer, but I knew what I had accomplished. My legs were sore, stiff, and living proof of the truth that I did indeed run twenty-six-plus miles in 6:32.

According to the official scorekeeper, I didn't finish the New York Marathon. But if you're scoring in the real world I definitely finished, and definitely kicked ass.

❄

Washington, D.C. is beautiful, but I was beginning to find it a bland, flavorless place. I was disenchanted by the political scene, and the charm of living down the street from the World Bank had completely dissipated. Everyone I met seemed to be a lobbyist or work on Capitol Hill, and I was ready for a change. New York had a vibrant vibe, an energy that was completely lacking in Washington, and I was ready to move back home.

One problem: I had zero job prospects, and you don't move to New York City without a gig. But fate intervened in the form of Paddy Rossbach. One week after the marathon, she left a message on my answering machine: "Hey, Sarah. Great job on the Marathon. I wanted to pass along a message I got from a woman at USC in Los Angeles, and she thinks you might be eligible for a scholarship for athletes with disabilities. How would you like to go to grad school for free? Call me."

Free grad school sounded perfect. I loved learning and really enjoyed my classes at G. W. (especially after I straightened up my act), so I wasn't ready to stop being a student. I never considered it, because the thought of taking out more student loans—and thus taking on more student debt—made my stomach hurt. But now, with only a month left until graduation, I was presented with an incredible opportunity to go to grad school. It would be the answer to dreams that I hadn't even dreamt.

I decided to let the fates decide. I'd apply at USC, and I'd apply for the scholarship, and if both of them came through, I'd go to California. With fingers crossed, I called Paddy, who put me in touch with Mara Redden from the board of the USC Physically Challenged Athletes Scholarship Fund.

The scholarship was started in honor of a former USC All-American swimmer named Mike Nyeholt. After becoming paralyzed from the neck down due to a horrible motorcycle accident, he lost his eligibility for his swim scholarship. Fellow teammate Ron Orr pulled together a fund-raising swim-a-thon, with the goal of raising enough money to help Mike pay for his tuition and a wheelchair accessible van, which would enable him to live independently and get around school. That eventually evolved into an annual fund-raising event called "Swim with Mike," and this scholarship program. Most of the athletes on the scholarship were people who'd become disabled later in life, e.g., the star high school quarterback who got hit by a drunk driver, or the star baseball player who broke his neck diving into a shallow lake. Using those criteria, I wouldn't qualify, but it was still worth a shot.

That night, I went to the school library online to find out what kind of programs USC offered. There was law school, med school, business school, a cinema program, and I was like a kid in a candy shop. Journalism hit me at a gut level— instead of being a politician who *tries* to generate change, I could be a writer who *succeeds* in generating change. All of a sudden, knowing there was the possibility I'd be able to get into one of these programs, the world opened up for me.

Two months later, in January of 1998, I flew out to L.A. and stayed in the Hollywood Hills with John Siciliano, an amputee friend who was going to USC on the Nyeholt scholarship. He was a gracious host and excellent tour guide. "I'll take you to some classes," he said, "and I'll take you around the campus, and the scholarship people are having a planning meeting, and you can meet everybody."

I loved it.

I loved the campus, I loved the California vibe, I loved riding around in John's convertible, I loved that I could run outside in a tank top and shorts in the middle of the winter, and I loved all the admissions people. It was a veritable lovefest, and I wanted in.

I interviewed for the scholarship, and I could tell they weren't convinced about me. Since I hadn't done a sport and then lost my leg, since I brought my disability to the table from the get-go, I was in a gray area. I suspect their thinking was along the lines of, *We're not really set up for somebody like her. Where does she fit?*

John spoke to one of the people on the scholarship board, who told John, "She's not exactly the kind of candidate we give our scholarships to. Yes, she was a high school track athlete, but that was after she became disabled; we fund athletes that were athletes before they became disabled."

John said, "She was seven when they amputated her leg. What kind of athletic career was she supposed to have? I know when she was six, she played in the town soccer league one season. Does that count?"

"That's not competitive athletics, and the amputation was because of a birth defect, so I'm afraid she doesn't fit the scholarship criteria."

I was deflated and disheartened. The window on grad school had closed, possibly for good. I had just spent a big chunk of change on this trip out to L.A., and maybe it had been for nothing.

The next morning, on yet another perfect seventy-two-degree California day, John took me for a ride around the city. I took in all the sights, resigned to the fact that I wouldn't be seeing all that much of L.A. in the immediate future. We'd been driving for an hour, when I spotted a mural advertising the Los Angeles Marathon right along the freeway, on the concrete wall by the 101/110 merger in downtown L.A. Stuck in traffic, I stared at this display, and the wheels started turning.

"Do you know when the L.A. Marathon is?" I asked John.

He shrugged. "I have no idea. Why?"

"Maybe I should run it. Maybe I could get people to sponsor me, and I could raise money for 'Swim with Mike.' I mean, I'm a terrible swimmer, but I know I *can* run. I truly am an athlete, and I would be a great addition to this school and scholarship fund, I just need to show them." John didn't seem entirely convinced by my plan, but he agreed to help me in any way he could.

The L.A. Marathon was in March, which gave me a whole two months to train. L.A. was going to be more difficult than New York because David wouldn't be able to run with me. But I'd finished one marathon, so I knew I could finish another. I blew the dust off of my NYC training schedule, bought some winter running gear, and got busy.

On race weekend, I flew back out to L.A. and crashed at John's place. I'd told the USC scholarship folks I would be running the marathon wearing a USC hat and a "Swim with Mike" t-shirt, and would also send in my pledges and donation checks after the race. I didn't know if it would nab me the scholarship, but I knew it wouldn't hurt and it was a good program to support either way.

About three miles into the race—which, just so happened, put me right in the heart of the USC campus—I came even with a reporter in a news truck who was interviewing some of the back-of-the-pack runners. I peered at him for a minute or two, thought, *Hmm, hmm, hmm, ahh, screw it, I'm going for it,* then ran up beside him and yelled, "Hey, I'm Sarah! I don't know if there are any other amputees running today, but I came all the way out here from New York to run the race on my artificial leg!" I felt a bit silly, but I needed all the exposure I could get.

The newsie smiled. "Hey, Sarah, I'm Tim McLoon. That's *awesome.* I've got to go interview these Marine guys . . . "—he pointed to a group of twenty-some-odd men wearing camouflage, running in a militaristic formation—". . . but if you stay to the left of the road, we'll catch up to you."

"Okay! Right on!" Once again, the squeaky blonde one-legged wheel got the grease.

Ten minutes later, Tim rolled over for a chat, and this wasn't going to be for a package that would run on the local 11:00 news; we were live. I was nervous and hoped I could actually speak and run at least somewhat gracefully at the same time. He had me introduce myself to the viewers, then asked me why I was running. I said, "I'm raising money for USC's 'Swim with Mike' scholarship fund, and we just passed the USC campus, and I'm so pumped to be running for a great cause." Tim then asked how I lost my leg, and a few other follow-up questions and that was it; it was all done in ninety seconds.

(I later found out that almost immediately after the interview, the scholarship people started getting phone calls, and the callers were all saying the same thing: "Ohmygawd, I just saw this girl on NBC talking about 'Swim with Mike', and she was awesome." My on-the-fly plan was a huge success.)

After Tim tossed it back to the studio, he turned to me and said, "No way!"

"No way, what?" I asked.

"You're from New York. So am I. And we need to exchange information, because my neighbor is a seven-year-old girl who wears a prosthetic leg. She's going through a tough time, and I have to connect you guys. I also work on the New York City Marathon show. Have you run that one yet?"

Now I'm not a big believer in fate, or destiny, or whatever, but there have been a few times in my life when something happened that shook my lack of faith. It turned out that meeting Tim was one of them. *Something* brought us together.

I finished the race in 6:15, and was shocked that in less than six months I'd shaved about fifteen minutes off my time. What with the television appearance and the money I'd raised, I thought the chances of getting a scholarship looked pretty good, so much so that almost immediately after I got back home, I booked a flight back to Cali for the big "Swim with Mike" event in April, so I could personally deliver the donation checks. That'd show 'em.

Mom said, "You're crazy. You're spending all this money that you don't have. What if they don't give you the scholarship?"

I said, "It's a risk I have to take. Think about it: I've spent about $1,000 on plane fares, and I might get a $50,000 scholarship. It's an investment. A speculative investment. And I love this school. I have to go there and swim with these people."

And I went. And they were thrilled that I was there, but they probably covered their eyes while they watched me swim, because I stunk up the joint. While I was in the water, I mostly clung to the wall as my friends John and Paul Martin swam their laps. I spent most of my time on the pool deck, where I met Mike Nyeholt, and schmoozed with Mara.

At that afternoon's barbecue, Mike Nyeholt's former teammate Ron Orr read off the list of names of the scholarship winners. When he said "Sarah Reinertsen," I had to keep my cool, because it wasn't the time or place for a demonstrative *Price is Right* kind of display. But inside, I was jumping up and down.

I wouldn't learn if I was accepted to USC for another month, but I thought my chances were solid; I had a decent transcript from G. W. and a good score on my GRE, but to put me over the edge, I included a TV news piece that I'd edited with the help of my mom's fiancé, a news reporter for one of the local New York television stations. It was a short feature that told the story of my life using old VHS footage and home videos. The application was good enough, and in early May, a couple weeks before my twenty-second birthday, I was accepted into USC's Annenberg School of Communication, and it was time to start packing up my life and moving out to the West Coast.

Soon after the beginning of my first semester, it hit me that the New York City Marathon was just around the corner. I'd done L.A. in 6:15, which meant I'd improved over fifteen minutes in only my second race, and I wondered if I could make that kind of leap again: So I went back home for a second round.

Tim McLoon was working the NYC Marathon, and when he heard I was running, he pitched my story to the team that was covering the race. This wasn't Len Berman and the local boys; this was the official national show that I'd watched back in Long Island.

They bit.

Tim told me they didn't have the budget to come out to California to shoot the story, but if I flew out to New York, it would be no problem. Since it would give me the opportunity to see my family and get some work done on my prosthetics, I booked a ticket that day.

And then, in a blink, it was race day.

Confident that I'd break seven hours, and not wanting to be disqualified again, I started at the official race time of

10:45. I had to weave and bob my way through the crowds, and Tim did a live interview with me running on the course at Fourth Avenue, after which they ran the pre-taped interview we had done weeks earlier. I couldn't have paid for that kind of publicity.

The race was my smoothest marathon yet. Less hop/skipping and more out-and-out, leg-over-leg running led to my fastest time ever; I crossed the finish line in 5:52, and I was stoked with the thirty-six minute improvement. (I can't take all the credit for the bump. A brilliant inventor named Van Phillips had just designed a foot for distance running called the C-Foot, now known as the Flex-Run. It was a huge technological advance, and I was lucky enough to get one of the prototypes.)

Back in Los Angeles, I fell into a nice groove. I was a good little grad student, making friends, getting good grades, and dating a guy from San Diego. (The dating thing was perfect, because a long distance relationship meant I'd only have to have a boyfriend on weekends, which left weekdays free for training and homework.) I was in great physical shape, probably the best shape of my life, and was looking for another big goal to conquer, because after four marathons, twenty-six miles was getting kind of boring.

My roommate was a fellow amputee track athlete named Jami Goldman. She was training for the 2000 Paralympics, and it set my brain a-spinning. *Maybe I'll try the Paralympics again. Maybe there will be enough women for us to have a full, fair race. Maybe I'll finally win that medal. Plus I've never been to Australia, so why not?*

It had been a good three years since I'd done any serious sprinting, and my short distance chops were a bit rusty, so training-wise, I had to pick up where I'd left off five years before. Training for sprints and distance are two very different animals. For long runs, you could pretty much slap on your shoes and go, but for short runs, you need someone to be hands on, to run the stopwatch, to keep an eye on your form, to tell you to "pump your arms, lean forward, have faster feet, only ten meters left, so come on!"

I couldn't fly to New York to work with David, so I figured I'd take advantage of what was probably the only logical resource available to me: the USC track team.

I popped over to track coach Ron Allice's office, poked my head in the door, and said, "Hey, I'm Sarah, and I've been doing marathons for the last couple years, but my background is in track, and I want to try and get fast again so I can go to the Sydney Games in 2000."

He said, "Sounds good. Let's do it."

Ron was amazing. He welcomed me as part of the team—he even got me a locker in the varsity locker room where I could leave my running leg and some shampoo. The whole thing made me feel like I was hanging out with the cool kids. It was a privilege to work out with the likes of Angela Williams, the only person in NCAA history to defend her 100m title for her entire four-year college career. I enjoyed the college track experience I didn't even know I wanted . . . *rah rah, Trojans!* (I have to admit I didn't wear USC track clothes, not because I lacked school spirit, but rather because dark burgundy and mustard gold don't look particularly good on me. I'm more into blues and pinks.)

I graduated in 2000 with a master's degree in broadcast journalism, and it was a melancholy moment. I was ready to leave academia, but over the past two years, I'd become an honest-to-goodness Trojan, who loved running on that USC track. Also, what with my great professors and multitude of cool friends, I knew I'd really miss the place.

A few weeks later, I went to Hartford, Connecticut, for the Paralympic trials, and, long story short, I didn't make the team. Yes, I was kind of bummed I wouldn't go to Sydney, but I picked myself up, and started looking for a job. And I got one. And I got to go to Australia, not as an athlete, but as an actual, honest-to-goodness professional journalist.

I landed a gig as a field producer for WeMedia, which was doing streaming Internet coverage of the 2000 Paralympic Games in Sydney. Olympic speed skater Dan Jansen was our reporter, and the two of us worked trackside in the Olympic stadium, covering six to ten hours worth of track and field a day. We also put together some video packages that were picked up for Fox Sports Network, and it was a ton of fun. It was also a ton of work; at one point, I went twenty-eight hours straight, without a real break. I could barely speak, and Dan thought my exhausted ramblings were hilarious. I have little memory of that day, which is no surprise, because by hour twenty, my brain was leaking out of my ear.

I knew it was going to be a short-lived position that would conclude when the Games were done. But when it ended, I was pretty bummed, especially since I had to start looking for a real job.

Fortunately, a real job came looking for me.

CHAPTER 5

ALWAYS TRI

In 1999, while I was still in graduate school, I was hired to do live human interest interviews with back-of-the-pack runners at the New York City Marathon . . . all while I was running the damn thing. The camera was on a motorcycle in front of me with the cameraman sitting backwards filming me running and interviewing the marathoners. Len Berman wouldn't be covering me anymore; he'd be my co-worker. The producers knew I'd completed four marathons and wouldn't have a problem keeping up with the crowd. Everyone from top to bottom was unbelievably hyped, myself included.

This in-field experience was invaluable, extremely fun, and extremely rewarding. I interviewed a breast cancer survivor who was running the marathon in honor of a friend who hadn't survived the dreadful disease. It was moving/amazing/incredible to share her story with the world as she pushed a wheelchair of pink roses along the course. This was a dream come true. The little girl from Long Island who'd watched a dozen marathons growing up was now one of the people on the course reporting the action from 1st Avenue at the NYC Marathon—*cool!*

In the television world, the majority of talent hunters

are often nervous about hiring a disabled person to do on-camera work, no matter how qualified or experienced they may be. Think about it: Are there reporters on your local news telecast who have one arm? Or who use a wheelchair? Doubtful. Some, however, can see past the disability; all they care about is performance, and know-how, and skills, prosthetic limbs be damned. Two of those people were Karen Demasi and Brian Williams, from a company now known as IMG Media.

※

The following year, I was out of work, crashing at friends' apartments in New York City, with no idea what to do next. And then, like manna from heaven, I got a call from Brian Williams, asking me to come by for an interview. I must've done well, because I was immediately hired as a reporter/producer for a thirty-minute nationally syndicated show called *U.S. Olympic Gold,* which was hosted by Olympic swimmer Summer Sanders. The show's format was simple; each episode consisted of four segments about athletes who were training to represent the United States at the Olympics. I'd be on-camera for one of the segments, and produce, or write, or edit some or all of the rest. It was hands-on, diverse, and dealt with a subject matter near and dear to my heart. Win/win/win.

Here's the basic job description: Fly around the country and interview Olympians, which, to me, was the most awesome job description ever. The timing for starting an Olympic-centric job couldn't have been better, because the Sydney Games had jazzed up the sports world earlier in the year, and we were only two years away from the Winter Games in Salt Lake City, so there were plenty of great stories and willing interviewees to choose from. It wasn't particularly glamorous—we had a shoestring budget, and it was all very D.I.Y.—but it was a blast.

My first assignment was to catch up with the U.S. speedskating team at their training facility in Butte, Montana. As much as I loved the job, Butte was a pain in the butt, the primary annoyances being 1) there weren't any direct flights from New York to Butte; 2) the training rink was outdoors, which meant I'd be standing in snow for virtually the entire shoot; 3) it was the middle of December, and the average December temperature in Butte was about three zillion degrees below zero; 4) having lived in California for the past two years, my cold weather wardrobe consisted of . . . nothing; and 5) I had to spend one third of my first paycheck on a serious winter jacket, a turtleneck, and long johns that would keep me cozyish during the aforementioned three-zillion-degree-below-zero weather.

Because of our lean show budget, we always tried to do two features at each location, and my first on-camera pieces were interviews with speed skater Derek Parra—who ended up winning a gold medal in Salt Lake—and speedskating Olympic couple Jennifer Rodriguez and KC

Boutiette. As the weeks progressed, I also produced pieces on super-cool skiers Bode Miller and Picabo Street, as well as sprinters Tim Montgomery and Marion Jones, a pre–*Dancing with the Stars* Apollo Ohno, and a very young, very shy, very sweet-natured swimmer from Baltimore named Michael Phelps. (A few weeks later, Michael blew off college and NCAA swimming, and signed a deal to become pro—but Speedo offered him millions for endorsements, so who could blame him?)

These were all fluffy pieces filled with softball questions, geared to show viewers how these athletes were living out their Olympic dreams. That being the case, in some ways, I was the perfect person for the job. My interview subjects were comfortable with me because I'd been there and done that, and my disability seemed to make them feel like they could open up to me, especially the notoriously media-shy Bode, who spent much of our chat telling me about how he'd spent a lot of time and resources helping out a boyhood skier friend who'd been paralyzed in a car accident. In some cases, my subjects turned the tables and started grilling me about my leg, my Paralympics experience, and my marathons. Believe it or not, my amputation made me a better journalist.

As the Salt Lake Games got closer, we started focusing solely on winter sports, and in some cases, the athletes we featured who participated in the less glamorous events were more of an inspiration to me than the big-name skaters or the skiers. For instance, the typical sports fan only pays attention to, say, bobsledding and luge once every four years, and it was so impressive to hang out with these people who'd given up a huge chunk of their lives to pursue a sport that would never earn them a great living, or public glory. All their sacrifices and hard work got me thinking about triathlons.

※

I suppose you can't be surprised that it was a military Commander who came up with the idea of the Ironman Triathlon. Commander John and Judy Collins had been living in Coronado when the sport of triathlon was born in the mid 1970s in San Diego on a small spit of land called Fiesta Island. When John was transferred to the island of Oahu in Hawaii a few years later, he and Judy got involved in a post-event discussion as to whom was the fittest endurance athlete: the runner, the cyclist, or the swimmer. John's solution? Since he had been exposed to triathlon in San Diego, he came up with the ultimate triathlon: combine the Waikiki Rough Water Swim (2.4 miles), the Around Oahu Bike Ride (112 miles), and the Honolulu Marathon (26.2 miles), and the winner would be proclaimed the Ironman.

So on February 18, 1978, fifteen guys went to a beach in Honolulu, dived into the ocean, and swam the 2.4 miles. Then they jumped out of the water and biked the 112 miles. Then they ran the marathon. Twelve finished. Everyone who finished received the Hole-in-the-Head trophy that was made personally by Commander John Collins.

Word got around, and the next year, another fifteen people showed up, including one woman named Lyn Lemaire. They didn't have race support, so the Ironmen-to-be stationed their family and friends all over the course, and gave them water and bananas to hand out to the participants.

In 1980, ABC's *Wide World of Sports* went out to Hawaii and covered the race, and that's when Ironman entered the public consciousness. The following year, there were 326 participants, then in 1982, that number jumped to 580. The '82 Ironman was particularly memorable thanks to the battle between Julie Moss and Kathleen McCartney. Julie outswam Kathleen by twenty minutes, they rode about the same, and then, during the marathon, Julie pulled ahead by almost twenty minutes. A few hundred yards before she hit the finish line, her legs gave out and she collapsed. She pulled herself up, then fell down again. And again. And again. Her legs were jelly. Eventually, she was able to walk/ run for about fifty yards, then she collapsed again. Again, she struggled to her feet and hurled herself forward, but thirty yards from the end, Kathleen passed her and won the race. Julie ended up crawling across the finish line.

Wide World of Sports showed the footage dozens of times, and as a result, Julie was invited onto all the night-time talk shows, where she was both doted over and told that she was crazy. Crazy or not, Julie Moss put the race on the global map. In 1985, an anonymous donor put up $100,000 for the winner. In 1986, there were 1,381 participants. Today, there are almost forty Ironman competitions around the world.

In 1985, a man with an artificial leg named Pat Griskus completed the Hawaii Ironman, and soon after that, a steady flow of one-legged males entered the race. It so happened that a number of these guys got their artificial legs made at the same place I did in Hicksville, New York. One afternoon in 1992, while I was at the shop waiting for the leg experts to finish the repairs on my limb—in one of the most amazing pieces of timing in my life—I flipped over to NBC, to the Ironman World Championship in Hawaii, and there's a guy named Jim MacLaren, plowing through the race in 10:42 . . . which, I now know, is an unbelievable time for someone with two real legs, let alone a racer with a prosthetic. He smashed the seemingly unsmashable eleven-hour barrier and set a new world record.

It blew me away. I thought, *Wow, the Paralympics are cool, but if you could do that, that's over-the-moon extraordinary. That's the bomb. I want to do that one day. No, I'm going to do that one day.*

I'm going to make Hawaii mine.

❄

One month after I was hired at IMG, I found a rent-stabilized railroad apartment in the Williamsburg section of Brooklyn.

Williamsburg was increasingly trendy, so the yuppies were taking over and gentrifying much of the neighborhood, but my block—with only two apartment buildings and six active warehouses—was one of the sketchier in the area, busy and smelly during the day, and barren and creepy after dark. It made me a bit nervous, but I was tough. This was New York so I knew I could handle the grittiness.

My building was a fourth-floor walk-up with a graffiti-covered front door and nasty hallways that were painted brown and beige and covered with a film of dust and dirt. The landlord completely neglected the building, and left the building super, Cubita, in charge. Cubita lived in the basement and was drunk 80 percent of the time, almost always too drunk to fix a leaky faucet, or unclog a clogged toilet, or clean up those nasty hallways.

But frankly, I didn't care. I had a huge, cheap two-bedroom apartment with a sweet living room and excellent views of the Williamsburg Bridge, the World Trade Center, and downtown Manhattan. As I watched the city twinkle each night, I began to believe that I'd be able to find my way in New York. I'd had roadblocks, but nothing stopped me, and looking at the skyline, my spirit felt invincible, like I was Superman, like I could leap over those buildings in a single bound.

But that was at night. In the morning, reality would hit me again as I had to face life as a working girl in New York City.

Yes, I had grown up in the New York area, but Manhattan

wasn't exactly Long Island, and IMG wasn't exactly Capitol Health, so it took me a while to get used to the grind. First and foremost, getting to work was a bitch. It started out with a twenty-minute walk from my apartment to the subway stop, which was okay on nice days, but a pain in the ass in the rain, or during the winter. Next was the train ride, which was an adventure unto itself. The L Train was so packed that some days, I'd have to let a few trains go by because there was no way for another body to smush into the car—even a tiny body such as mine. Since I was too short to reach the strap or bars overhead, if I didn't get a seat, I'd have to "Subway Surf," i.e., keep my balance on the train ride while holding onto nothing. Even for the able-bodied, Subway Surfing takes a lot of balance and core muscle strength—it should be an Olympic event, for crying out loud—but for a short chick with a prosthetic leg in a high-heeled shoe, forget it.

And then there was the matter of stairs. Between climbing up and down the stairs of my walk-up apartment building, and the four flights during my subway transfer, I walked six hundred stairs a day. Now I can't walk up the stairs leg over leg, so it takes extra work for me to go up, but going down is truly an athletic feat of balance and rhythm. My daily commute became part of my training. Who needs a Stairmaster when you're doing twelve hundred steps a day, five days a week?

It was a hard life, but I was still basically a happy girl. With my cool job and cool apartment in a cool (albeit ghetto-looking) neighborhood, I became a semi-prototypical single chick in New York. Not *Sex-in-the-City*-wear-fabulous-clothes-and-date-a-guy-like-Mr.-Big single, mind you, but rather go-out-on-the-periodic-lame-date single. But that didn't stop me from trying to meet my own Mr. Big.

Even though I'd gotten more comfortable with removing my prosthetic in front of a guy I liked, the disability sometimes made things a bit awkward. For example, if I was at a bar, and I hit it off with a guy, and I was wearing jeans, and he couldn't see my legs, it wasn't like I was going to tell him, "No, I'm not limping because I sprained my ankle, I had my leg amputated when I was seven. So my friends and I are going out dancing now. You wanna come with us, or what?"

Mom told me time and again that my leg would weed out the bad guys, but sometimes I'd meet somebody who had a decent job, and lived only three subway stops away, and wonder, *At what point do I try and weed him out?* There was no right answer, nor will there ever be.

Sometimes the whole thing got flat-out awkward for everybody involved. For instance, I was out on a first date with a cool, cute guy who didn't know about the amputation—it was winter, and I wasn't wearing anything that offered any clue, and I hadn't broached the topic. He took me to a movie, we sat down, and half an hour from the end of the film, I looked down and noticed that his hand was resting on the thigh of my leg. My left leg. My fake leg. I had no idea how long he'd been feeling me up, and I had no idea how to ask, and I had no idea when I should tell him, or *if* I should tell him. (I ended up spilling the beans later that night, and he just laughed and blushed, so it was all good.) If I had thinner skin, the whole thing would've bummed me out pretty badly. But there were three-plus million guys in New York City, and there was probably one for me.

Another *Sex and the City* issue: shoes. I didn't have a fancy-schmancy Heather Mills cosmetic leg that I could adjust to match the height of my shoes; my "office leg" had a stagnant heel that measured exactly two and three-quarter inches, not a size all that common at Macy's or Nordstrom's. All of which meant I had to carry a tape measure with me whenever I went shoe shopping and measure each heel. Sometimes that meant going to five, six, or seven shoe stores. Now multiple trips to multiple shoe joints are some women's ultimate dream. For me, it was a pain in the instep. Every shoe expedition turned into a treasure hunt, and I ended up hating them.

Shoes and boys notwithstanding, life was good. I was in New York, and I had a career, and I was on TV, and it was all worth it. I learned so much about television production, I had great friends in the city from high school and college, and supportive colleagues at the office, and life was humming along. It was an exciting time, and I was in a good space, so I knew that it was as good of a time as any to start on new endeavors of my own.

One word: Ironman.

Step one: Learn how to swim.

❈

There aren't too many public swimming pools in New York, but, in a brilliant stroke of luck, there was one located a couple blocks away from my Brooklyn apartment. I walked by the place day, after day, after day, and finally, at the start of 2002, worked up the courage to sign up for a pool membership.

Before I jumped into the water, I needed to gear up, so the day after I got my pool pass, the day of my first swim, I treated myself to a swimsuit shopping spree at an adventure store near Union Square. I bought a one-piece racing swimsuit with tropical flowers—because that way whenever I put it on, I'd think about Hawaii—a matching swim cap, and a pair of goggles. I was set.

As I approached the pool building for my first training session, I thought: *Sarah Reinertsen, you are going to look so cool in your cute little bathing suit, and your cute little swim cap . . . but wait a minute . . . you're going to have to take off your leg at the pool. Where are you going to leave it? Will it be safe in the locker? Would somebody steal a prosthetic leg? It is New York, so it's certainly possible. Do you rest it near the edge of the pool where you can keep an eye on it? If yes, is there anywhere to leave it where it won't get wet? How busy is the pool going to be? And who'll be there? Will you see that weird guy from the L train, the guy who always tries to look down your shirt? Why didn't you think about any of this before you spent all that money on your gear and your membership?* This wasn't the kind of stuff that Summer Sanders or Michael Phelps ever had to worry about. By the time I reached the doors of the building, I was so freaked out that I walked home, and consoled myself with a pint of Ben & Jerry's Coffee Heath Bar Crunch.

This went on for almost six months; I'd pack up my swim clothes, walk to the pool, and walk right back home. Whenever I went by the place on the way to and from the subway, I felt a twinge guilty, remorseful, and a little spineless—and I went by that pool *constantly.*

Finally, in the midst of one of my many training jogs, I gave myself a pep talk: *Sarah, you have this dream of doing an Ironman. If you think you can dive into the ocean and swim 2.4 miles, you have to at least be able to get into the neighborhood pool. You can't let fear and embarrassment stop you from achieving your dreams.* It stuck. The following Saturday, with a new sense of clarity and purpose, I mustered up the strength to go to the pool.

In a daze, I went into the locker room, put on my cute little suit, dumped my street clothes in the locker, and stepped out to the pool deck, wearing my prosthetic. I walked over to a metal chair by the far wall, sat down, slipped off my leg, hopped over to the pool, and dived in as quickly as possible. I didn't need anybody gawking.

I did two laps, and about halfway through lap number one, it hit me: *Holy shit, 2.4 miles in the ocean might be a little more difficult than I thought.* But I didn't let it daunt me; 2.4

Sarah Reinertsen, born on Long Island, NY, in May 1975 with a tissue disorder known as proximal femoral focal deficiency, making her left leg shorter than her right leg.

FROM SOLVEIG FUENTES/ DON REINERTSEN

Sarah Reinertsen, age 8, in the hopping race on field day at Flower Hill Elementary School in Huntington, New York. This was the one event she could win a medal in at school, hopping better than just about everyone.

FROM SOLVEIG FUENTES/DON REINERTSEN

Sarah Reinertsen, age 7, getting fitted for her first prosthetic leg after amputation. She now gets her prosthetics made at A Step Ahead Prosthetics on Long Island, and it's almost still the same process—she gets a mold of her stump over a silicone liner, completely custom and handmade. Then the hardened cast is removed to create a unique mold for the socket.

FROM SOLVEIG FUENTES/DON REINERTSEN

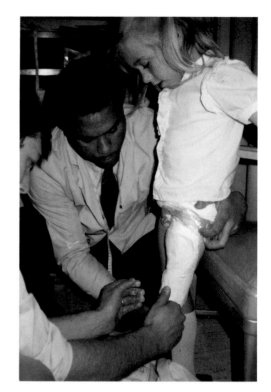

Paddy Rossbach and Sarah Reinertsen (age 12) at Mitchell Field Track for the Empire State Games for the Physically Challenged. Paddy is a below-knee amputee, and is the first endurance amputee runner Sarah ever met. Paddy took Sarah to her first track competition, told her about the Paralympic games, and ignited her passion for running.

FROM SOLVEIG FUENTES/DON REINERTSEN

Sarah Reinertsen, age 22, on the podium in Duderstadt, Germany, as the 1997 Paralympic Revival Champion for the 100m, above-knee amputee women (T42). Sarah also broke a world record at that meet, beating out Jo Astley (AUS) and Christine Wolf (GER), who are pictured on the podium. It was the start of Sarah's comeback in running.

FROM SARAH REINERTSEN

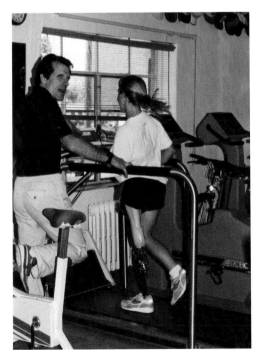

Sarah Reinertsen, age 17, running on the treadmill at David Balsley's physical therapy gym in Colorado. David Balsley, an ultra-marathon runner and PT from New York, taught Sarah how to run and coached her for many years.

FROM DON REINERTSEN

Sarah Reinertsen, age 13, skiing a gate course at Mt. Sunapee, New Hampshire. Sarah grew up skiing in New York and New England with family and friends after taking lessons in an adaptive ski program as a child.

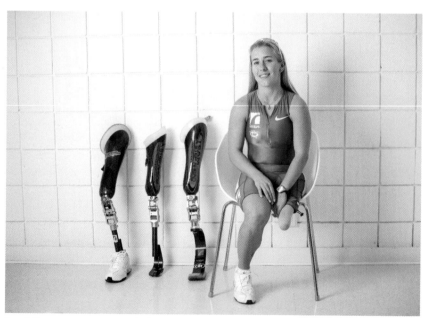

Sarah Reinertsen, age 32, with the prosthetic legs she uses for triathlon, from left to right, the walking leg, the cycling leg, and the running leg (including the Flex-Run running foot). Sarah works with Ossur to develop the best prosthetic technology for both living and sport.

Sarah's family, from left to right: step dad, Pete Fuentes; brother, Peter Reinertsen; Sarah Reinertsen (center); dad, Don Reinertsen; mom, Solveig Fuentes; step mom, Joan Reinertsen. One of the greatest victories of Ironman was bringing her family together.

Sarah Reinertsen waiting for the 2003 Pat Griskus Triathlon to start. In 1985, Pat Griskus became the first man on an artificial leg to do the Hawaii Ironman; this sprint triathlon in Connecticut is held annually in his honor.

Sarah Reinertsen climbing the cliffs of Ha Long Bay, Vietnam, on season 10 of the CBS hit reality show The Amazing Race. *This episode won an Emmy award for best reality series in 2006.*

Sarah Reinertsen and Peter Harsch running through Kuwait for season 10 of the CBS show The Amazing Race. Sarah and Peter ran a good race but lost it literally in Kuwait and were eliminated from the race hours after Sarah climbed the tower in the picture.

Sarah putting on her prosthetic leg after the swim portion of the Timberman Triathlon. Sarah doesn't wear a prosthesis for the swim so she must be met as close to the shore as possible with her leg, so she can quickly put on her prosthesis for the next portion of the race.

Sarah off for a transition run—when you immediately go for a run after riding your bicycle. You can see her bike propped up on the garage in the distance. She has it all set up so all she has to do is park the bike, throw on her run leg, and go. She does like to have her iPod to get her going on these T-runs—when you just want to stop moving, the music won't let you.
FROM DON REINERTSEN

Sarah riding her custom-made bike, called SASSY1, also known as "Unfinished Business." It was the bike the Cannondale team made for Sarah to ride in the 2005 Hawaii Ironman.
FROM DON REINERTSEN

was just a number, and I wasn't going to let some stupid number quash my goal. Besides, after making it through the front door, past the locker room, all the way to the side of the pool, and into the water, 2.4 miles was nothing. That said, after my two laps, I got the hell out of that water and went the hell home.

For my next water training session, I decided to go the David Balsley route, and not worry about distance, but instead time. Come hell or high water—or, in this case, overly chlorinated water—I would stay in that damn pool for five minutes. If that meant one lap and hanging on the side for four-and-a-half minutes, so be it. If that meant eight laps, so much the better. I couldn't let myself get bogged down by the numbers one way or the other. My primary goal was getting comfortable in the water.

I knew I'd eventually have to get more than just my sea legs (or, I suppose, sea leg), which meant I'd have to figure out the right way to swim. I knew how to freestyle, but not particularly well; I was all arms, and energy, and big splashes, and heart. Freestyle is all about pulling and glid-ing, and I wasn't doing much of either. My motions were completely inefficient, so I expended a ton of energy and got nowhere. I felt awful for the poor people at this tiny five-lane pool who got stuck sharing a lane with me, the girl who resembled a water-bound bumblebee.

Friday after work became my official swim day, pri-marily because A) the pool was far less crowded than it was on the other weekdays, and B) they cleaned the pool on Friday afternoons, which meant there wouldn't be any old Band-Aids floating around the shallow end. I didn't go every single week—life does get in the way—and the Fridays I didn't go, I punished myself by not going out all weekend. On the other hand, if I went when I *really* didn't want to go, I'd allow myself a brief get-together with my two favorite sweets purveyors, Ben and Jerry. (A brief aside: During marathon training, I'd periodically forego an ice cream bowl, throw away the lid, and down an entire pint of Half-Baked. Before you get all repulsed with my gluttony, remember that one pint is only two cups, which, when you think about it, isn't *that* much. I'm just saying.)

I wasn't obsessed with triathlons—I wasn't yet a card carrying "tri-geek"—but they became a constant presence in my life. I'd buy *Triathlete* magazine once every couple of months, and I played the Ironman broadcasts on my VCR on a semi-regular basis. My friends, however, would probably tell you that I was a total geek, because I used to make them watch those tapes constantly. "This is going to be me someday," I'd tell them, as we watched Tim DeBoom and Natascha Badmann cross the finish line. They all thought I was crazy, but they supported and believed in me, so they didn't make fun of me. Much.

In spite of the fact that I wasn't taking swim lessons, my swimming slowly began to improve, which I credited to simple repetition; the more I swam, the better I swam. Best of all, each week, I was able to do more laps in the same amount of time. One Friday, it was ten laps in ten minutes, and after a few weeks after that it was fifteen laps in ten minutes. If I was going to do those 2.4 miles, I had to at least be able to be comfortable in the pool for twenty-four laps, so there was still a long way to go.

I read lots of books about swimming, so I learned the theory behind good swimming form, but the actual execution in the pool was another matter. Then there was the issue of straightness. One of the questions I'm often asked is, "If you're only kicking with one leg, do you swim in circles?" The answer is, not really, but I have to do a lot of compensating to go forward; if I stop paying attention, there can be a fair amount of zigzagging. Eliminating the zigzag is vital because as we all know, the shortest distance between two points is a straight line, and I needed to make sure that the 2.4-mile jaunt in the Pacific didn't become a 3.4-mile torture. Also, as I learned in *Triathlete* magazine, it's important to use your arms as much as possible during the swim, because you need your legs to be as strong as possible for the run and the bike ride.

And speaking of bikes . . .

※

Every weekend in Brooklyn, there are approximately 1,205 stoop sales, where bargain hunters such as myself try and find hidden treasures, like a nice jean jacket, or a nonstick pan, or a used-but-usable piece of exercise equipment. Like, for instance, a mountain bike.

What with all my triathlon research, I'd learned that tri-bikes start at $1,500, which didn't fit into the budget of a low-to-mid-level television producer who was paying off tons and tons of student loans. Besides, I didn't even know how to ride, so how could I justify spending two-plus months' rent on something that could wind up being used as a coat rack?

So it seemed like divine intervention when, one sunny Saturday afternoon in spring of 2001, I stopped at a sidewalk sale in Williamsburg, hosted by a woman who was about five feet tall. Now why is that important? Because I'm five feet tall, and I'd fit perfectly on the cute little mountain bike she was peddling.

I examined the bike from top to bottom. It was white-framed, with new knobby tires, and fluorescent highlights of pink, orange, and yellow paint graphics splattered all over it. It looked a bit 1980s, but she said it was only a couple years old, and she'd used it when she was in college, but she didn't ride much in Brooklyn. I didn't really care about any of that, because it was my size, petite, feminine, and perfectly fitted for me. "How much do you want for it?" I asked my fellow short chick.

She shrugged. "Hundred bucks?"

I said, "Will you take seventy-five?"

She shrugged again. "Sure. Cool. Why not?"

"Great!" I gave her my last five bucks and said, "Here's a down payment. Where's the nearest ATM?"

I walked my new bike home about two miles, then hauled it up my four flights of stairs—not a simple task, because mountain bikes are frigging *heavy*—and I rested it against the wall of my kitchen. After staring at it for a few minutes, I said aloud, "All right. This is the bike I'm going to learn how to ride on. Pretty soon, I'll be *totally* ready for Ironman."

The next weekend, I hauled the bike down the four flights and walked it to my neighborhood bike shop, where I loaded up on gear—helmet, shorts, clip pedals, the works—and got a tune-up. Then I walked it home, hauled it back upstairs, and leaned it up against the wall in my kitchen . . . where it remained, untouched, for approximately one full year.

It got to be an annoying space-taker-upper, so I bought a big hook and hung it from the kitchen ceiling—it looked like Jerry's apartment in *Seinfeld*—where it collected lots of lovely New York City dust, and absorbed all kinds of lovely Sarah Reinertsen cooking smells. Not very Ironmanish, but what are you going to do? The bike hung from my ceiling, taunting me, dangling like a dream that was both literally and figuratively out of reach.

One evening after a particularly good swim, I stared at the bicycle and thought, *I can swim over twenty minutes without stopping, and I can run a marathon with my eyes shut, so I'd better get moving on this bike thing.* The 2002 Winter Games had come and gone, I had watched so many of the athletes I interviewed achieve their Olympic dreams, and it was time to take action on my very own Ironman dreams.

It dawned on me that I'd been procrastinating because I was scared. Yes, I had a helmet, and the toe clip pedals, and the bike was in good shape, but this was New york City, and you can barely walk across the street without getting smeared by a taxi. A one-legged, ninety-five-pound girl who didn't know how to ride a bike wobbling down the street would be an easy target. I had the enthusiasm and heart to cycle, but as is sometimes the case with me, I didn't quite think things all the way through.

I realized I was in over my head, and I had to ask for help. Thing is, I'm not good at asking for, or accepting, help. But sometimes you have to, so I went back to the bike shop and said to the most sympathetic-looking clerk, "Hi, I'm Sarah, and I'm training for the Hawaii Ironman, and I don't know how to ride a bike. Do you guys give lessons?"

The poor guy was perplexed. "You don't know how to ride a bike?"

"Correct." He looked at my leg.

"And you want to do Ironman?"

"Yup."

"Ooohkayyyy. Um, what kind of bike do you own?"

"I have a mountain bike."

"You're going to do Ironman on a mountain bike?" He rolled his eyes.

I rolled my eyes right back at him. "No. I need something to learn on. So do you give lessons, or what?"

"No. We don't." He paused, then asked, "Do you spin?"

"Spin?" I had no idea what he was talking about.

"Yeah. Spin. You go to your gym, and you get on a stationary bike, and you ride for an hour, and it's really intense."

Now I didn't belong to a gym, just the pool, the New York Road Runners Club, and the Williamsburg Track Club. (By the way, yours truly was the creator of the Williamsburg Track Club, which consisted of me and five of my girlfriends, all of whom I had to bribe to run, i.e., "If you guys do three miles with me, and watch one of my Ironman tapes for the millionth time, I'll buy you dinner and beer.") Only a handful of my friends had gym memberships, and none of them had ever mentioned anything about spinning, so I was clueless.

He said, "Okay, you don't have to take a spin class, but maybe we could set you up to spin at home."

"How?"

"We could stick your bike on an indoor trainer, and you could practice in your apartment, so your legs can get stronger, and you can get more confident, and then when the weather's nice, you could take the bike out to a parking lot and practice."

That was genius. Not only would I be able to get in riding shape, but I could figure out how to rig my prosthetic to the bike with the toe clips. "Let's do it." Three minutes and $300 later, I was the proud owner of a CycleOps trainer.

I put the trainer in the living room, right in front of the TV. The bike came down from the hook. Once it got set up, it *stayed* set up.

And then I rode.

And rode.

And rode.

I wasn't going anywhere, but I was moving toward those 112 miles.

I fell in love with the bike, and would hop on almost every night after work. As was the case with running and swimming, it was about how long, not how far. I started out doing ten minutes, then twelve, then fifteen, then twenty. When it got to the point that I was able to ride for an entire episode of *Seinfeld*—commercials included—I was thrilled. I soon evolved from sitcoms to hour-long dramas, to full-length movies.

But for the rest of my New York City life, that bicycle never once left my apartment.

❀

At the beginning of 2003, after almost three years on the job, IMG laid me off. The economy was a bit of a mess, and they had to let a bunch of people go—nobody was safe; higher-ups and lower-downs were all getting whacked—but they liked me, so I made it until the third round of cuts. That didn't cushion the blow much, but it's always nice to be loved.

For the next four months, I collected unemployment, job-hunted, swam, and biked. Exercising was essential, because it kept me focused on Ironman, plus I couldn't afford to do anything sociable, so if it weren't for working out, I'd have been a complete disaster.

Physically, I was in great shape, but emotionally, not so much. Being unemployed is one of those stressful life things like death or divorce. I felt lost and purposeless, because it was hard not to connect my self-worth to my job, but I did, and when I didn't have a job, there wasn't much for me to cling to, except for Ironman.

My bike and the pool were my twin lifelines. I could turn a bad day into a good one if I turned the pedals for an hour, or drowned my sorrows in the pool. In between training sessions, I e-mailed and faxed my resume everywhere I could think of and called every contact I knew in hopes of finding a new job.

Since the 2004 Summer Olympics in Athens were still eighteen months away, there were a few nibbles ("Keep in touch with us, we might need a freelancer in Greece"), but nobody had anything solid. While I managed to get a couple freelance gigs, I couldn't find any full-time work, so I continued to work out regularly.

Despite the strides I'd made toward Ironman, I felt myself slipping back into depression. I slept later and later, because what was the point of getting up early if I didn't have to be anywhere in particular? And all my friends were at work, so I had nobody to hang out with, so why not stay in bed?

And then in March of 2003, I received a mass e-mail from the Challenged Athletes Foundation in San Diego. I'd worked with the C.A.F. on a number of different levels for ten years; I respected the hell out of their work, and they respected the hell out of mine. They were looking for a program manager, someone to oversee their grants and sports clinics. The C.A.F. was a nonprofit organization, and it wasn't exactly a huge conglomerate; the program manager was one fourth of their entire staff, so they needed to fill the position fast. Twenty minutes after I fired my resume over, Tabi King, their director of development, called me up and asked, "Are you really applying for this job, Sarah?"

"Yes."

"Really?"

"Yes."

"Really?"

"Really."

"Um, why? Aren't you doing all that big fancy TV stuff?"

"Not anymore." I filled her in on my layoff, and the frustrating job hunt, and, of course, my Ironman training.

Tabi said, "Why would you want to work here?"

"Well, I believe in the cause, and even though it's not journalism, it's still sports related, and I could also make a difference in the world with you guys. My last job was to cover the stories of athletes, now I can help athletes. Plus I want to get out of New York. I love it here, but I went to grad school in Los Angeles, and I can train all year round. It's like the sunshine and palm trees are calling out for me. And there are bike lanes in San Diego, so I can actually ride outside. And you guys have lots of clean pools, so I don't have to swim with Band-Aids . . . "

"Band-Aids?"

"Don't ask."

"Okay. But I don't think we'll be able to pay you what you were getting at IMG."

I said, "Probably not, but I'm getting *nothing* now, so *anything* is a step up." On that note, Tabi offered me the job.

I had no money, and I still didn't know how to ride a bike on the road, but moving to California put me that much closer to Hawaii, and thus that much closer to becoming an Ironman.

CHAPTER 6

I'MUA

In 2004, after doing triathlons for twelve-plus months, I decided I was ready for that year's Ironman, but it wasn't the kind of thing where I could show up in Kona and say, "Hi, I'm here, what time do we start?" In order to qualify for Hawaii, I had to first complete a Half-Ironman competition—a 1.2-mile swim, a 56-mile bike ride, and a 13.1-mile run—so that June, I went to Lubbock, Texas, home of the Buffalo Springs Lake Half-Ironman Triathlon. I specifically chose Lubbock because it's extremely hot—we're talking upwards of one hundred degrees—just like Kona. Also like Kona, the course they mapped out was very hilly. It's a tough, tough Half-Ironman, but I figured if I was going to prepare, I'd *prepare*. I needed to do something tough in order to become something tough.

Cutting to the chase, I finished. I earned my spot. I felt great.

NBC, who was covering that year's Hawaii race, heard about me, and decided to put together a feature on the first woman with an artificial leg to compete in Ironman. They came out to California and shot footage of me training; then they followed me to Kona, and made me one of their special interest stories for the race telecast, which would be broadcast the following Saturday. (Ironman is a looooong race—the elite professional men finish in eight hours, and the pro women in nine—and, knowing only a tiny number of people would watch the whole thing, NBC edits the highlights into a ninety-minute show.)

Almost immediately after I arrived in Hawaii, I was summoned to the Keauhou Beach Hotel for a pre-race interview with the network. They'd turned one of the hotel ballrooms into a mini-studio, and set up all these metal sheets to create this cool industrial backdrop. The whole process took almost an hour, and right before they wrapped, I stared right into the camera and said, "No matter what, I'll get to that finish line."

All the attention helped my confidence, and I needed all the confidence I could get, because succeeding in Ironman is 50 percent mental. You can be in the best shape in the world, but when it's eighty-five degrees, and you're riding your bike uphill against thirty-mile-per-hour winds, you have to force your body to keep moving forward, even when your muscles are screaming, *STOP*. There were instances in other triathlons where I'd had to walk, or run, or hop, or jog to cross the finish line, and I was prepared to do it again. I was going to make it through Kona . . . even if I had to crawl like Julie Moss.

My entire family came out to Hawaii: my mother and her second husband, my father and his wife number three, and my brother Peter, as well as my friends Heather, and Tabi from the C.A.F. Both of them are runners, and though they're not fanatic uber-athlete tri-geeks, they had a good idea of what I was going through.

This was the first time my parents had spent any significant time together since their divorce, and there was most definitely some tension; my mother was there with both her ex-husband and her current husband, so how could there not be? I mean, there were eight of us—including my Dad and stepdad—sharing a rented duplex. Talk about awkward. Everybody was extra-polite to one another in my presence, but who knew what was happening when I wasn't around? Fortunately, they all realized that for the sake of my sanity, they had to at least appear to be a team. As a matter of fact, for the sake of team unity—and so I'd be able to pick them out in the crowd—I made them all matching bright green fluorescent shirts to wear on race day.

The race kicked off at 7:00 a.m., but the condo was a ways away from the starting line, and there's only one road you can take to get there, and it was a single lane, so I had to wake up at 4:30. It was pitch black, but even though the sun hadn't risen, it was hot, even at that hour; we're talking eighty degrees, and sticky humid. I padded over to the tiny kitchen in my room and threw together a small bowl of oatmeal with a little banana and guzzled down an electrolyte drink called Cytomax. (A quick note to all you aspiring triathletes: You don't want to eat too much breakfast, because it'll sit in your stomach like a rock when you're swimming, but you still need a little bit of fuel, so eat something. However, don't worry about starving during the race, because you'll get to eat while you're riding the bike, and before you start the marathon. Here's my secret food weapon: Pringles. They're super salty, and all that salt helps you retain water, and since you're going to sweat out *everything*, you'll need all the salt you can get.)

Tabi and I drove down to the parking lot of the King Kamehameha Hotel—the starting point and the place where we'd left our bikes the day before—and there was absolutely no place to park. Little surprise, because you're dealing with two thousand racers, and their friends and families, and volunteers, and race officials. So I pulled up to the attendant, reached under my seat, whipped out my handicapped placard, and said, "Excuse me, sir, do you have any handicapped spots available?" (The irony of an Ironman participant asking for a handicapped spot wasn't lost on anybody.) We nabbed the space, then Tabi grabbed my biking and running legs—I could've carried them, but why waste the energy hauling twenty pounds worth of legs when I had a sixteen-hour day ahead of me?—and we were on our way.

Step one of Ironman is the body marking. This is when a volunteer puts an I.D. chip on your ankle, then stamps your race number on your arms and your legs with a semi-permanent ink—after all, you can't wear a paper number in the water. (I was number 187, which, it so happens, is the Los Angeles police code for a homicide. I'm still not sure whether or not that was a good sign.) The majority of the racers' numbers were beige, but a few had orange digits.

The oranges were the people whom NBC was going to follow. I was an orange.

When the camera crew noticed my number, they swooped in and they cranked up their lights, and it was still dark out, and it was like, *Whoa. Showtime. Gotta be cool. Be brave. Be graceful.* I was used to being in front of the camera, but I was nonetheless a little bit freaked out, because I was about to do something I'd never done before, and there was always a chance something could go wrong, and nobody wants to have egg on their face on national television. It also brought home the gravity of the situation. It wasn't merely just me showing up and giving this thing a shot. The NBC crews were going to capture every single second. From that moment on, I had a camera with me almost the entire time.

After I was fully body marked, I made my way over to my bike and gave it a pre-race once-over, which was essential, because the temperature had cooled down a little bit overnight, so my tires weren't at the optimum level of 120 psi I made sure the bike was in a nice, easy gear so I could get off to a good start after I got out of the ocean, I filled up my water bottle . . .

And then I went blank.

I was in robot mode. It wasn't by design; it just happened. I was still functional—I remember wishing the other racers luck, and giving some people an "Aloha" or two—but they were just words. I was hollow and detached. I watched the scene from outside of myself. I couldn't stop thinking, *I'm here, I'm at the Hawaii Ironman Triathlon, I'm here, I'm here.* "Right Here, Right Now," a tune by Fatboy Slim, and part of the unofficial Ironman soundtrack, was pumping through the sound system. The energy and the media madness were amping up—there were helicopters filled with cameramen shooting from the sky, and video-toting divers shooting from the bottom of the ocean, and almost one hundred lifeguards on surfboards and paddle boats on both sides of the course. The dark sky had broken, and it was getting lighter, and lighter, and lighter, and it was 6:45, time for the professional racers to kick off their swim. Their starting cannon went off—it wasn't a small gunshot, it was a big boom—then the ocean was a blur of white foam, and then it was time for us amateurs to get into the water.

The Hawaii race has what's called an in-water start, as opposed to triathlons where they shoot off the cannon while we're on the sand, and then we run into the ocean. The beach starts are a colossal pain in the ass for me, because I have to hop long stretches through the sand to get to the water. Soft sand is difficult to hop in because I sink, and once I sink, I have to hop harder, and it wears me out. But for the in-water, I could swim out to my position, then tread until the cannon, just like everybody else.

In order to conserve energy, I sat down on the folding chair that Tabi had been hauling all over the island. As the crowds of racers got thicker, I removed my artificial leg, gave it to Tabi, then hugged her goodbye. When we separated, it was like somebody had clipped my umbilical cord; I realized that I was going to be more or less alone for the rest of the day. Yes, there would be people everywhere—racers, cameramen, officials, volunteers—but really, I was on my own.

Once in the water, I shed my mental robot armor and crawled across the ocean bottom until the water was deep enough to swim in; there was more crawling involved than hopping, because too much hopping either in or out of the water trashes my good leg. As I watched all the amped racers slowly swim the one hundred meters to the starting line, I kept telling myself, *You've done your training, it's going to be okay.* I repeatedly meditated on the Hawaiian word for "keep moving forward"—*i'mua . . . i'mua . . . i'mua . . . i'mua.*

I stayed back from the pack a bit. I'd become a good swimmer, but I was far from the strongest one out there, so I knew I wasn't going to finish the race in an hour, like the elite swimmers; I figured I was looking at a 1:45 time, so it made more sense for me to hang behind everybody. I didn't want to get into a boxing match for position. I wasn't trying to win. I wasn't interested in the prize money. I just wanted to finish.

Most everybody near me was frantically treading water; it was a sea of pumping legs. Me, I lay on my back and floated, and relaxed, and gazed up at the sky for the next ten minutes, and it was such a moment of peace and tranquility. And then right at 7:00 a.m., the cannon went off. Peace, gone. Tranquility, gone. It was time to swim. I hit the start button on my watch, and off I went.

There were problems from the get-go. One of the other swimmers accidentally kicked me in the face and knocked my goggles out of alignment. I swam over to one of the lifeguards on the surfboards, grabbed the plank, readjusted myself, and coughed out the saltwater I'd sucked in. I then got back into the flow of swimmers, but I made it a point to avoid feet. One kick was enough.

I knew I had to be patient with the swim. I was going to be out there for almost two hours, and that's a ton of time—it's about how long it takes to watch, say, *Chariots of Fire*—so I tried to quickly find a groove and a comfort zone. I got kind of Zen about the whole thing; I whittled the process down to the basics: *stroke, breathe on the right, stroke, breathe on the left, stroke, breathe on the right, stroke, breathe on the left.* Next thing I knew, I'd gone almost 1.2 miles. Halfway home.

We made our turn back to shore around a boat that was crowded with fancy V.I.P.s and super race sponsors, all of whom were partying, and hanging out, and drinking Bloody Marys and beers, all cheering us on. It was pretty cool, all that excitement and yelling way out in the middle of the ocean. As I cruised around the boat, I started taking breaths only on my right, so I could keep watching them, keep drawing on their positivity. They didn't know who the hell I was, and I didn't recognize a soul, but they still gave me an awesome jolt of energy.

After leaving the boat in my wake, things got hard. The current and the swells were pretty rough going out, but they were *really* rough coming back. Almost every time I turned to take my left-side in-breath, I got smacked in the face by a wave and sucked in another mouthful or three of saltwater. And thanks to all of those choppy swells, I started feeling kind of seasick.

I pushed, and pushed, and pushed, but the pier wasn't getting any closer, and I thought, *Oh my God, when am I gonna get there?* It had been an hour-and-a-half, and I wasn't just physically tired—I was tired of swimming, sick of the Pacific. It crossed my mind that it might be a good idea to reverse my course, make my way back to the party boat, and get a couple of drinks.

All that said, I was getting closer to the next stage, so I had to get my mind right. I had a bike ride and a marathon to come, and I had to step it up, but I still had to be smart about it, and keep a smart pace. I had to remember not to kick too hard with my right leg, because it messes up my line. I had to be as even, and smooth, and symmetrical in the water as I could, so A) I didn't overcompensate and start drifting; and B) I still had enough leg strength left to make it through the ride and the run. The swim is the only sport where you *really* use your arms—sure, you pump them some when you're running, and you have to hold yourself up with them while you're on the bike, but I wasn't particularly concerned. The legs were the issue. So, looking longingly at the beach, I thought, *Come on, Sarah, one stroke faster. Use your arms. They can recover on the bike. Let's . . . get . . . this . . . swim . . . done.*

Suddenly, a guy pulled up to my right on a surfboard. He cheered, and yelled, and screamed encouragement, and that was a huge help. Several hundred meters from the shore, I was hit with a wall of crowd noise, and I needed it. The roar got louder, and louder, and louder with each stroke. It was a veritable siren song, welcoming me, inviting me out of the water, and cementing the fact that I was a third of the way to becoming an Ironman. The pier to get back onto dry land was less a pier than it was a boat ramp, and it was lined with spectators, as well as a couple dozen race workers, two of whom pulled me onto the ramp and gave me my crutches. (Remember, I had a long day still in front of me, and I wanted to keep my hopping to a minimum.) I crutched my way toward a tent at the end of the ramp that housed a few overhead showers—and thank God, because after almost two hours in the Pacific saltwater, I was crusty and in need of a *serious* rinse.

They had a chair set up for me past the tent at the end of the pier, so I could sit down and put on my leg after I got out of the shower—I didn't want to put it on beforehand, because there was a chance that it might not get dried properly, and would rust up while I was out on the course. (Unlike 99 percent of the other triathletes, I had to always be mindful of little things like that.) Plopping myself down on that chair wasn't as magical as you might've thought, because I knew it was critical that I not get too comfortable. I didn't want to give myself over to that feeling of *ahhhhhhhhh,* because if I did, there was a chance I wouldn't get back up.

So I slapped my running leg on as quickly as I could which, unfortunately, wasn't very quickly. It takes me about twenty seconds to put on my leg in my house when I get out of bed, but when I do it after a swim, it takes longer, because my fingers are all pruney, plus I'm all adrenalized and jacked up. I wanted and needed to rush, but my hands were fumbling. I felt like I was moving in slo-mo. And then there was the issue of sea legs. After bopping around in the water for almost two hours, my lower body was in a jelly-like state. It was probably a mere fraction of what poor Julie Moss's legs felt like at the end of her tragic, courageous run, but it was still bad.

I went to the top of the pier, grabbed my "187" bag, and made my way over to the women's changing tent. I didn't put on a new outfit—I did the bike wearing the same white jersey and bike shorts I'd worn in the ocean— but, with the help of the amazing volunteers, I put on some new socks, a bike shoe, and tons of SPF 30. (I made the fatal mistake of forgetting to put on lip block. My lips got so sunburned that the next day, I could barely speak.) I then had to run about two hundred meters to the parking lot to get my bike—remember, there were two thousand racers, and you can't keep all their bicycles at the end of the pier, because that would cause a nasty traffic jam—where one of my handlers was waiting for me with my bike leg and a chair. I tore off my running leg, slapped on the bike leg, clipped myself onto the pedals, thanked everybody profusely, and rolled off.

I turned the corner out of the parking lot and then *boom,* Pualani.

Pualani is a brutally steep hill that takes you out of town. It was tough—we had to loop around and do it twice, actually—but then I caught a glimpse of a group of people wearing bright green fluorescent t-shirts, and, well, seeing my family and friends made that hill feel that much smoother. After Pualani, we did a ten-mile jaunt through town, where the streets were lined with cheering crowds, and I was pumped. The swim was becoming a memory.

But then I made a left onto the Queen K Highway. It was literally and figuratively the turning point.

The Queen K is the only major road in Kona, and it's as desolate as the surface of the moon. There are black lava rock fields on either side of the highway reflecting the sun, making it feel far hotter than ninety-five degrees. It's you, and the road, and the sun, and the heat, and that's it. Forty-six miles out and forty-six miles back. And you see nothing except for the heat rising from the pavement. No grass, no trees, no shade. *Nothing.*

For me, in general, riding the bike is a meditative experience. Ideally, I can find a gear that feels like cruise control. iPods are illegal in Ironman, so sometimes I sing to myself—Madonna's "Ray of Light," or "Cecilia" by Simon and Garfunkel, or a Beatles song, or, of course, the Black Sabbath triathlete anthem, "Iron Man." It's the karaoke hour. It's a mental mix tape. Anything to keep myself happy. Anything to keep myself going.

I'mua . . . i'mua . . . i'mua . . . i'mua.

Even though I was a good distance away from most of the other riders, I wasn't living entirely in a vacuum. Once in a while, a person or three would come to the end of the driveway of the resort they were vacationing at and give me a wave and a cheer. Sometimes a still photographer would pull in front of me on his chauffeured motorcycle and snap a few shots. And sometimes, the NBC crew would cruise alongside me and ask for a status report.

I'd been on the Queen K for about an hour, when I thankfully hit the second water tent, which was like an oasis. Aside from water, the tents offered Gatorade, bananas, and energy bars. After I fueled up and got back on the road, one of the NBC convertibles fell in beside me and the guy in the passenger seat yelled, "How're you doing, Sarah?"

He was one of the guys who came out to film me during training, so I yelled back, "I'm feeling great, Dave! I'm in Hawaii, man! I've got a beautiful view of the ocean, and the lava rocks, and it's awesome! I'm almost twenty miles into the ride here, and I'm wondering when those Kona winds are going to kick in!" (I should probably mention that Kona is a Polynesian word for "leeward," and "leeward" is a nautical term for "bad downwind." This means the town was named after a dangerous breeze.) I shouldn't have said anything about the wind, because I think Lono, the Hawaiian god of weather, heard me. And apparently I pissed him off.

Five miles later, the headwinds started. Up to that point, I was cruising along at eighteen miles per hour, which, based on the math I worked with during training, would get me off the course in plenty of time. But when that wind kicked in, my speed was halved, and I had a mild freak-out, because I knew the Ironman numbers up and down. You see, a triathlon isn't merely a matter of swimming, and biking, and running, and then putting on your medal and your official I-am-an-Ironman t-shirt. You have to finish each race within a certain time frame. For the Hawaii Ironman, the swim had to be completed in 2:15. If you come in at 2:15:30, you're done—no bike, no marathon, just a trip back to the King Kamehameha Hotel. You had to complete the bike ride by 5:30 p.m., and I knew I'd need to maintain a fourteen mile per hour average to make that happen.

I was happy with my speed up to that point, so in spite of the slowdown, I wasn't really concerned. My thinking was that since I had headwinds going out, I'd have tailwinds coming back, and I'd make up the speed, and I'd be cool.

At the thirty-five-mile mark, a good ten miles away from the turnaround in a hilly town called Hawi, I was still getting wrecked by those headwinds, but I still didn't stress. *It is what it is,* I thought. *It's all part of the Ironman game. Save your legs for that big climb leading into Hawi. I'll finish the incline, I'll get my Pringles at the food tent, and I'll have a downhill run and the wind at my back. It'll be totally cool. I'mua . . . i'mua . . . i'mua . . . i'mua.*

Now I may be a better swimmer than some of the other racers, but once they get on that bike with their two legs, well, suffice it to say that I'm used to getting passed when I'm going uphill. On the incline up to Hawi, there were a whole lot of people yelling "ON YOUR LEFT," then drifting over to the right, then a whole lot of them flying on by. But it was all good, because my time splits were still looking good. Sort of. I did some quick calculation and realized that if I was going to make the cutoff, I wouldn't be able to stop for *anything.* And *anything* really meant *anything,* which included going to the bathroom. And that meant I'd have to urinate while riding. I timed it so I peed after a water stop, which gave me the opportunity to dump a cup of water over my head and disguise the mess. Turns out I shouldn't have been shy about the situation, because I found out later that pretty much everybody pees on their bike.

Finally, I hit the Hawi hill, and at that point, half of the racers were already on their way back to town. I was one of the few stragglers still on the climb. I was watching my watch, and my speedometer, and was well aware that the sand was moving through the hourglass. I needed to be off the bike at 5:30. It was almost 2:30. I had to make fifty-six miles in three hours. I had to have the ride of my life.

Right at that moment, it wasn't looking good. I was going uphill. The headwinds had picked up. And I was cruising along at a jaunty four miles per hour. That's how fast a typical person walks to the grocery store. But I couldn't go any faster.

Fortunately, the turnaround was within sight, and I couldn't have been happier, because my "special needs" bag was mere minutes away. This is a bag that you can fill with all kinds of fun goodies—food, a change of shirt, anything within the Ironman rules that will help you get through the rest of the ride. You check it in the morning before the race, and they'll bring it up to the Hawi hill so it'll be up there, waiting for you, ready to give you a push. I was dying to have at my Pringles, my gummi bears, my Red Vines licorice, and a camelback water container filled with a mixture of H_2O and Carbo-Pro. Carbo-Pro is flavorless, but it adds calories to your drink, and I figured out during my training that I needed to consume between one hundred and two hundred calories an hour to keep myself properly fueled up. Thank you, Carbo-Pro.

I grabbed a few yummies from my bag and headed downhill. A few hundred yards of struggling later, I thought, *Dude, you're still pedaling pretty hard here. You're not going that much faster than you were before the turn. Maybe this downward grade isn't as steep as you thought.* I looked at my speedometer—eight miles per hour. Yes, I had doubled my speed from when I was going up the hill, but I was still just under half of where I needed to be. I thought with the wind and the hill, I'd be speeding along at twenty miles per hour.

What happened was, the wind kept shifting. And it picked up. And shifted. And picked up. From hard headwind, to swirling sidewind. But no tailwind. Fuck you, Lono.

There were barely any people left on the course—after all, this was the world championship, and the elite people were *very* elite, and thus long gone. There were practically no rabbits up ahead for me to chase. I had to dig deep, and stay focused, and stay strong. I had to take it one hill, one turn, one lamppost at a time.

Around 3:00 p.m., the crosswinds mellowed, but, as is the case virtually every afternoon in Kona, the tradewinds made their entrance, and I was again freaked out. Since I was out on the course longer than I expected, I was forced to pour down more Carbo-Pro; I ended up taking in about 350 calories an hour, and that was far too much. Around the seventy-five-mile mark, my body started to reject the calories, which meant vomiting. I'd drink a little, then *ble-ahh,* I'd throw up, then I'd drink some more, then *bleahh,* I'd do it again. I was getting concerned about dehydration—if I couldn't hold liquids, I couldn't replace what I was sweating out. There were more than twenty-five miles to go, and I had to keep myself hydrated, especially since after I got off the bike, if you'll recall, I was going for a little bit of a run.

Right after my fifth vomiting session, a blue SUV sporting race credentials on the dashboard pulled up beside me. It was Tabi and a race spotter who'd been assigned to track me down. They both started talking at me in unison: "Hey, Sarah, how you doing, you're doing great, way to go, keep it up, yay Sarah!"

The Queen K had all these rolling hills that I hadn't noticed while I was driving in the car, plus the tradewinds were getting worse by the minute, so my speed was yo-yoing between eight and fourteen miles per hour . . . and I could never break fourteen. I couldn't do it. It wasn't going to happen. I looked at my watch (again), then my speedometer (again), then I stared at Tabi for a second and said, "I'm losing time. I don't think I'm gonna make it. *I'm not gonna make it.*"

Tabi leaned out of the window and said, "Sarah, you *are* gonna make it. You're gonna do fine. Hang tight. Keep riding. Keep pedaling. We're gonna run some numbers, and figure out what you need to do." Then they pulled ahead, and I was alone again.

I wanted to cry, but I was too dehydrated. My quads screamed at me, but I didn't listen. I just kept pedaling and singing my songs. I tried to concentrate on the ground right in front of me so I wouldn't get frustrated staring at the never-ending horizon ahead.

I caught up to them five minutes later; they drove slowly alongside me so I didn't have to stop pedaling. Tabi said, "Okay, Sarah, here's the deal: You need to average sixteen miles per hour between here and the finish line if you want to make it. And you *can* do it. You *will* do it."

I'd consistently done sixteen miles per hour in training, so I knew it was possible, and knowing there was a chance was unbelievably invigorating. I had hope. I *could* do it. I *would* make it. I looked at the speedometer (again), and I pedaled and pushed and pulled as hard as I could. I gave it everything I had. Normally during the bike section of a triathlon, I hold back 1 percent, because I might need it for the run. But if I didn't hustle, if I didn't give it *everything,* there wouldn't be a run. So I went balls out.

I pedaled and pushed some more, all the time staring at the speedometer: twelve . . . thirteen . . . fourteen. . . . Sometimes I'd hit sixteen, but I couldn't hold it. I started thinking about Lance Armstrong, and the Tour de France, and those guys that can pedal one hundred miles a day for an entire month, and their pain, and how much their quads must hurt, and how they made it through those insane hills in the Swiss Alps. And if they can do it, I can do it. I used every mental and physical tool at my disposal to pull every ounce of my strength.

I pulled my speed back up, hovering around fourteen, fifteen, and sixteen, but all of a sudden, *bleahh,* I puked again. Tabi and the spotter pulled up and said cheerfully, "You're looking great, Sarah! How're you doing? You're looking strong!"

I said, "Yeah. I'm doing fine. But here's the thing: Every time I puke, I've gotta slow down. I'm having a little trouble figuring out how to keep up my pace and puke at the same time."

They looked at each other, then Tabi turned to me, grinned, and said, "All right! She's back!"

But really, I wasn't.

I never gave up hope. I stopped looking at my watch, and started chasing the sun. But it was dropping. Fast. Tabi and the spotter figured out well before I did that I'd lost too much ground, and I wasn't going to make it by 5:30.

As I got closer to town, I finally admitted that I was going to fall short, so I started thinking, *Maybe for TV's sake, they'll let me do the run. Maybe they'll give me, like, a five-minute grace period. Maybe I'll still be okay.* But deep down, I knew that the likelihood of that happening was slim to nil, so I got pissed: *How many mornings did I wake up at 5:00 in the morning to go to the pool, then go to work, then go to the gym again at night? All that hard work could not have come down to this.*

I was aware the Ironman pros had finished the entire race hours ago, and they were all at their hotels, kicking back, having a beer. I knew there were probably a good number of amateurs still on the course. But once I caught a glimpse of some racers running the marathon, my heart sunk; those bipeds were at the fourteen-mile mark of the run, and I was still on my bike, impossibly behind schedule. I clung to the hope and positive vibes from the other athletes. Those runners were so awesome. They yelled stuff like, "Way to go, cyclist! You got it! Come on, 187! You can do it! Keep it going!" It softened the blow. But not much.

Then, literally right at the moment the media caught up to me, I looked at my watch for the first time in a while: 5:35.

I was done.

The cameras followed me, and I tried to keep a poker face. I tried not to cry. I also tried not to throw up, but unfortunately I wasn't able to stop myself on that one. Luckily, when they showed me on television, they cut away before I puked.

When I got to the bike-to-run transition area, there was a huge crowd waiting for me. My family was there in their green shirts. Three of my sponsors from Cannondale were in the middle of the road, on their knees, raising their hands above their heads, then bowing down to me, a la *Wayne's World*. It made me smile despite myself. I loved that they were honoring my effort, but it didn't change the fact that the effort fell short.

I wanted to be an Ironman. All those years of training, and working, and believing in myself, and I was fifteen minutes short.

I unclipped myself from the bike, sat down on the folding chair the volunteers had waiting specifically for me, and I completely lost it.

Tabi ran over and said, "You did it! You're awesome! You did it, Sarah! You did the bike ride!" But the only thing I could hear was the loudspeaker at the final finish line. When everybody crosses the finish line, Mike Reilly, the official voice of Ironman, says, "John Smith, you are an Ironman!" All I could think was, *Fuck. He should be saying, "Sarah Reinertsen, you are an Ironman!"*

A few minutes later, my friend Bob Babbitt wandered by, put a Hawaiian lei around my neck, and gave me a hug. A race official soon came over and, without any ceremony, said, "Ma'am, we need to take your timing chip. Can I take your chip off your ankle now?"

He took it off, and that was it. I was officially out of the race. It was devastating.

It never occurred to me that I wouldn't do it, so I was shell-shocked. I was stunned. My family was stunned. My friends were stunned. After all, I'd defied the odds so many times that everybody assumed I'd always be able to triumph. I did too. My expectations for myself were enormous.

I was also totally embarrassed. The cameras were right there the whole time. They documented me crying, and sweating, and puking, and probably peeing.

Because I'd thrown up so many times, I was taken to the medical tent, and they made me sit there for twenty minutes while they nursed me back into shape. When I was finally hydrated to their satisfaction, I was allowed to go be with my family. They hugged me, and supported me, and if they weren't there, I don't know what I would've done.

We all went to the finish line and watched all those other people become Ironmen, and that was hard for me to take in. After a few minutes, I turned to my mother and said, "We need to go. I need to go home. Now."

Today, I honestly believe that not finishing the race was one of the best things that ever happened to me. I now know we learn some of our greatest lessons through failure. Of course I was bummed that I didn't become an Ironman my first time out, but I knew I couldn't wallow. I had gotten this far, and was closer to my dream than ever; there was no way I was stopping now. But in that moment, it was awful.

The only thing I could do was *i'mua*.

CHAPTER 7

MY AMAZING RACE

Peter Harsch and I met at the San Diego Tri Challenge in 1999, and it was interest at first sight. He was a certified prosthetist who made limbs for us amputees, but he was also a triathlete, who, like me, had been dreaming of doing the Hawaii Ironman for a good long while. He was a good-looking, athletic guy—tall, blond, metrosexualish—who made artificial legs for a living. The fact that he was a prosthetist was perversely appealing, and played no small role in my attraction to him. I mean, how cool would it have been to date a guy who could make me a different leg for every pair of shoes that I own? He could also make me a more diverse batch of sports legs, not only running and biking, but one just for climbing, or wind surfing. Also, unlike many other prosthetists I'd seen, he wasn't old and wrinkly.

In 2005, I moved to Orange County, reentered the corporate world, and took a job as marketing manager at a company that manufactures prosthetics, braces, and supports called Ossur North America—and who was Ossur's West Coast clinical prosthetist? None other than Mr. Peter Harsch.

Not only was it nice to have a pal at the office, but he was also a fine resource for good places to train in the area. I valued his friendship, and part of me still held out hope that the two of us could make a good pair. But he always seemed to have a girlfriend when I was single, and vice versa, and perhaps if the cosmos had been properly (or differently) aligned, we might've coupled up. But as it was, we were work- and work-out-buddies, and that would have to do for the time being.

John Siciliano, my old friend from "Swim with Mike," is an incredible athlete, and one of the toughest amputees I know; he's run numerous 10Ks and half-marathons, all while working as an actor in Los Angeles. Plus he trained with David Balsley, and you have to be tough to make it through those nutty Balsley workouts. He's also always up for an adventure, so he was a perfect candidate for a show like *The Amazing Race.*

John and his girlfriend Bridget had applied to be contestants on season ten of the CBS reality show, and, after cutting through miles and miles of red tape, they made it through the grueling selection process and were invited to be on the show. Unfortunately, Bridget's bosses at work mumbled and grumbled about giving her the time off to do the race, so, only one week after accepting the offer, Bridget and John backed out.

However, John still wanted in. But he needed a partner, preferably somebody with an interesting backstory who would pique the producers' interest. Maybe, possibly, another amputee athlete. Enter yours truly.

I loved the show, and, for the past couple years, had made idle threats to apply, so when John called me up and asked me if I would consider doing *The Amazing Race,* it was one of those this-is-meant-to-happen moments. I told him I'd love to, then he asked a vital question that few of the other teams on the show even have to think about: "Do you know how to drive a stick shift?"

This was a major issue, because between the two of us, we only had two working legs, and if you do the math, that's exactly how many legs it takes to handle stick, and most of the cars in the foreign countries the show visits don't have automatic transmission. I hadn't tried driving a stick shift in ten years, but I knew it was doable, so I told him, "Of course I do! It's easy! No problem!" I was only fudging a little.

The next day, John and I had a phone interview with the show's production staff, and they must've liked what they heard, because they asked if I could drive up to their offices in Los Angeles for a face-to-face meeting . . . immediately. Within a couple of hours, armed with the official Sarah Reinertsen press kit, some DVDs with video footage of me from various races and television broadcasts, and some still photos from Ironman, I was driving north on the 101 through Hollywood, imagining how John and I would tackle *The Amazing Race.* I knew we'd be a great team, because we were both strong runners and cyclists, and I spoke solid Spanish. We'd figure out the stick shift thing later.

And then, just like that, I'm at the *Race* production office. Natalie, the casting maven, pored through my clippings and pictures, smiled, and asked, "So how long have you and John Siciliano been romantically involved?"

I said, "What're you talking about? We're not dating. Bridget's been John's girlfriend for years, we're just friends."

"Oh, we thought you guys were dating," Natalie said. "All the other parts are cast, and we need a dating couple." She pulled out one of the still photographs from my pile. "Who's this guy? He's cute."

"Oh, that's Peter Harsch," I said. "Now there's a guy I should partner with. We're both Ironman triathletes, and we work at the same company, and he's got the skills to fix my leg on the race, and we're great friends, and we'd be a good team."

"Are you guys dating?" she asked.

"Er, not really."

"What does 'not really' mean?"

"Well, we've always wanted to date, but, um, the circumstances were never right, we worked at the same office up until a couple months ago." I then gave her my most ingratiating smile and said, "But who knows what'll happen down the line?" My performance was kind of lousy, and I had a hunch that the producer knew on some level Peter and I weren't into each other, but our respective athletic backstories were so compelling that Natalie asked me to see if Peter was interested, and that they'd go from there.

Peter was on a business trip in Texas. I called him on my way home from Hollywood, and he was a mess—turned out he'd just broken up with his girlfriend. (Now how's that for timing?) After he cried on my cellular shoulder for a few minutes, I told him, "I've got just the thing that'll cheer you up."

"I could use some good news. What's up?"

"How would you like to go on *The Amazing Race* with me?"

"Um, say what?"

"You and me. Partners on *The Amazing Race*. Next season. But here's the thing: They think we're a couple. So we're going to have to give an Oscar-caliber performance at our interview tomorrow."

"Tomorrow?" he asked.

"Yeah. Tomorrow. CBS is flying you to Los Angeles. So get your ass to the airport, and get to L.A., and start pretending that you're way into me."

When we arrived at the CBS headquarters the next morning, the receptionist guided us to a conference room, where we waited for our final meeting with the CBS executives. Peter and I sat in a big room, with another potential team consisting of a bilateral leg amputee from Las Vegas, and her boyfriend—apparently that year's *Amazing Race* was going to feature someone with a lost limb, no matter what—and a couple of network types whose job it was to keep us from interacting with one another. Being a sociable sort, I'd tried to say a friendly hello to my fellow amputee, but the CBS staff wasn't having it. We sat in silence for twenty minutes, then we were shepherded into another boardroom, where we delivered our "Vote for Sarah and Peter" speech.

We were warned that we'd only have two minutes to sell ourselves to the CBS execs, so, just to play it safe, we honed our pitch down to thirty seconds each. They sat the two of us on a sofa on the far end of a huge, rectangular room, facing a circle of chairs, all filled with different men and women staring at us awaiting our spiel. Before we could say a word, one of the CBS-ers said, "Okay, guys, we have one open slot, and we have to fill it, like, yesterday, because this rodeo starts next month. Why should we send you two?"

I talked about how we were both perfect contestants for this race, how we'd been training our whole lives for an opportunity like this, and how Ironman had more than prepared us for the challenge. I also mentioned that Peter was the perfect partner because he could fix my leg on the course. Then Peter chimed in with why I would be the perfect amputee to take on this challenge, and that he was proud to also get the opportunity this time to spend time with me and get to know me in a whole new way. We delivered our little semiscripted pitch almost perfectly.

It spurred questions from a few of the executives, and I knew that was a good sign—had they not been interested in us, they would've said, "Thank you very much, we'll be in touch." We walked out of the room feeling confident that we'd done the best we could, that we'd made a good impression. Peter and I high-fived in the hallway, and we could barely contain our excitement on our drive back home to south Orange County. But we tried to remain cautious; CBS hadn't picked us yet, and there was still so much of the race application paperwork we had to complete before a final decision could be made.

Before they could give us an answer, we had to jump through a few hoops: get a physical exam from both our personal physician and a CBS contracted doctor, submit to a series of psychological and personality tests, and go through background checks. We also had blood and urine tests, and we had to get all of our travel shots up to date (hepatitis A and B vaccines, Japanese encephalitis, etc.). They wanted to be sure we were of sound body and mind to go on this world adventure, so Peter and I patiently took all the tests and waited to hear the verdict from the casting office.

Five days later, while at Trader Joe's bagging up some groceries, my cell vibrated; it was somebody from the CBS casting department. All she said was, "You got it."

And right there in the middle of the checkout line, with four people waiting behind me, I yelled, "OHMIGAWD! YOU JUST CHANGED MY LIFE. I'M BUYING SOY MILK AND APPLES RIGHT NOW, THE SAME AS ALWAYS, BUT EVERYTHING IS DIFFERENT!!!" I was thrilled because I was getting to go on this crazy, once-in-a-lifetime, international adventure. This was something beyond anything I had ever really imagined, so out of reach that I never *truly* considered it, and now it was about to happen. I floated out of that Trader Joe's.

I treated the *Race* like a triathlon, which meant a whole lot of training. Unfortunately, I only had one month to prepare, and being that the whole point of the *Race* is dealing with the unknown, I wouldn't be able to work on anything but the most basic of basics. One of the things that I most often saw *Race* contestants doing was running around the streets of some random town carrying a heavy backpack. So each morning before work, I'd take a backpack, fill it up with dirty clothes, strap it over my shoulders, and trot around the neighborhood. My neighbors had watched me train for Ironman, so they weren't surprised to see me hauling ass up and down the street. When somebody asked why I was jogging around with the pack, I'd tell them, "There's this race in North Carolina, and it's an adventure race, and I'm getting ready for that." (That race really existed. I wasn't allowed to tell anybody that I was going on *The Amazing Race,* so I had to come up with a cover story.)

Probably the most important part of my training was the research and reconnaissance. I bought two copies of all the *Amazing Race* DVDs that were available, one for me and one for Peter, then I called him up and said, "I'm putting these in the mail. Study them. Look at what the contestants are wearing. Look for little tips and cheats. Figure out how we can get a psychological edge. And don't blow this off. If we're doing this, we should do it right."

Peter said, "Okay. But I have a confession to make."

"What's that?"

"I've never seen the show."

I sighed. "Forget regular mail. I'm FedExing you the discs. You'll have them tomorrow morning. And get your butt in gear. We leave for the *Amazing Race* in two weeks, and you need to be ready, because we . . . are . . . going . . . to . . . win . . . this . . . thing."

I wasn't just giving him lip service. We had the athletic strength, the street smarts, and the determination, so I honestly believed that the only thing that could keep me and Peter Harsch from winning the one million dollar prize was me and Peter Harsch.

And man, was I right.

⁂

After I scaled the Great Wall of China, all of us racers were fed a warm meal, and given a ride back to our hotel and a piece of advice: *Even though it's 2:00 in the afternoon, you should probably go to sleep, because dinner is at 10:00, and you're leaving for the next task at midnight, and who knows when or if you'll be seeing a bed anytime soon thereafter.* (A note: Part of what makes *The Amazing Race* so appealing for viewers is the interpersonal drama, and the more tired and out-of-sorts a contestant is, the more likely he or she is to either snap, or reveal a part of his or her true self that he or she hides from the real world, which is why they mess with our sleep cycle, and give us food only after the pit stops.)

Our next stop was Ulaanbaatar, Mongolia—it's the capital of Mongolia but still a very remote place—which meant dealing with a whole lot of rinky-dink, uncomfortable train riding through the barren Gobi Desert, over thirty-six hours worth of sand and nothingness.

We were given sleeper cars, so we could stretch out and catch up on some Zs, but the quarters weren't conducive to resting . . . especially when your partner leaves the window open overnight during a sandstorm. When we awoke in the morning, Peter, me, and all of our gear were covered in sand, and we were coughing up debris from the Gobi. Peter's hair looked like straw, and my prosthetic leg looked like it had been left out in a snowstorm.

There was no food on the train—we're not talking Amtrak here, with amenities like lunch for sale—a problem, because the last meal had been a bowl of rice at the train station in China over a day ago. (After our rice meal at the train station, Peter decided that we deserved a beer and bought one from the vendor in the station. I thought it was frivolous to waste our money on the beer; we could need the money later in the race, so I didn't drink much of it in protest. But I realized that was silly, as he'd already purchased it, and now I regretted not guzzling more of that alcohol down before this interminable train ride.)

But here's the frustrating thing: None of this was shown on television. Nobody found out that we were stuck in a tiny sleeper car with a couple of other contestants, and nobody was aware that one of said contestants left a train window open overnight and everybody in the general vicinity woke up with a chestful of desert sand. As far as the viewer knew, our ride from China to Mongolia was a breeze. The general public wasn't aware of our sleep deprivation, or our lack of nutrition. Nobody knew that when I broke down in tears in front of a camera, it wasn't because I was Ms. Sarah Softie Whinertsen, but rather because I was malnourished and exhausted.

What seemed like three jillion years later, we arrived in Ulaanbaatar. Our assignment: Hop into a jalopy and drive ninety-plus minutes to a city called Terelj. Easy, right? Wrong. Mongolian has nothing in common with any language I'd ever dealt with, so navigating through a city with exactly zero useful signage is a major problem.

Even though we couldn't speak the language, I was never nervous about getting harassed by the locals, or carjacked, or mugged, because we had a stealth security force watching our back. Wanting to make certain that none of their contestants got kidnapped and held for ransom by a Mongolian reality show hater, CBS hired a couple of security men from Control Risks, an international company that farms out former retired military men as bodyguards. And the Control Risks guys were badasses, special ops and undercover men who'd done covert work all over the world, e.g., Somalia, Panama, and the Middle East. Both of them were supercool, and had our backs.

Even with the language barrier and the heinous car, we were the first team to show up at a barn. A barn filled with horses. Leaving the comparative safety of the jeep behind us, we mounted our horses for a two-and-a-half-mile ride to the site of our next challenge. It wasn't exactly easy, but I loved riding through the stunning countryside on horseback.

Once we parked our horses, we were told to choose one of two tasks: Tear down a traditional Mongolian hut and then tie the hut's woolen blankets to a camel using a bunch of convoluted knots, or haul jugs of water back and forth while using a yak as your method of transport. From watching old episodes of *The Amazing Race*, I knew that wild animals are unreliable and unpredictable, so I figured it would make more sense to work with the camel, because we wouldn't have to get him to move from one place to the other.

Dealing with the camel wasn't that difficult. Dealing with Peter was a different story.

What with the way my father behaved when I was growing up, I'm pretty good at handling unstable alpha males, but when Peter started clapping at me as if I were a dog, or telling me that he couldn't move forward with me until I cooled out, or nastily berating me about keeping my mouth shut and focusing on the task, I tried to shut down, to not let it get to me. I knew all too well the emotional places he was going to, and I wasn't going to be dragged there. I wasn't going to live under anybody's thumb, especially with a million dollars on the line.

Being a media savvy girl, I was always aware that the cameras and microphones were on us constantly, and I refused to get into it with him; when I vented, I'd do it in the hotel, away from the production teams and the cameras. If he didn't realize how he was going to come off on television, that was his problem. So I shut him out as best I could, and went about the business of blanketing the camel—which ended up going so badly that we switched to the yak task. And it pissed me off, because I *hate* quitting.

Unfortunately, our yak was a lunatic—it's possible that Peter freaked him out—and absolutely refused to do what we needed him to do, so before we knew it, we were in last place. So it was back to the camel, which *further* pissed me off. But this time, in spite of the fact that I was crying, and dizzy from exhaustion and hunger, and covered with camel spit, I refused to stop. We spent a total of six hours tying that frigging blanket onto that frigging camel. The Mongolian camel herders who were chaperoning the camels saw what I was going through, and I could tell they felt sorry for me. Truthfully, I felt sorry for me, too.

At the end of the day, it all didn't matter, because despite the heinous car, the insane yak, and the antsy camel, we won this leg of the race, thanks to Peter. He totally redeemed himself at our next task when he channeled his inner Robin Hood and shot a flaming arrow into a teeny tiny target about a zillion yards away. For a brief while, I forgave him for his behavior at the river . . . but I certainly wouldn't forget that at the drop of the hat, he could shift into jerk mode.

Actually, it was impossible to forget, because Peter Harsch, in his inimitable style, kept reminding me.

❄

And then, Hanoi. With $33 in our pocket. I made it clear to Peter that nobody on our team would be buying any nonessential items (i.e., beer) when we got to Vietnam.

First stop, the Hoa Lo Prison, aka the Hanoi Hilton, which war buffs know was where the Vietnamese kept hundreds of their POWs; today, it's a museum that houses such memorabilia as the flight suit that John McCain wore while he was imprisoned. The directions for our next task were hidden somewhere in the Hilton, but, in the first of many problems that day, the museum wasn't open yet. Our second problem: We were immediately told that it's illegal to loiter or sleep on the street in a Communist country, so it was off to a hostel. Third problem, the hostel where we were told we could get some rest and have a meal was missing two essential components: beds for the contestants, and food other than stale bread and warm water. We slept on the floor, in the open atrium of the hostel, while fist-sized cockroaches scurried across the floor, and I went to bed without eating any of the stale bread. All eighteen of us contestants shared a single, gross bathroom. It was like being in prison. Thank you, CBS. (I should note that none of this prison stuff made it onto television. That said, I think that putting us in prisonlike circumstances was the whole point of the day, because the clue was hidden by that John McCain flight suit, and they wanted us to experience a taste of what Senator McCain had gone through.)

The clue at the Hanoi Hilton directed us to a flower market in the middle of Hanoi, where we were given one of our sillier tasks: hawk flowers. We hustled as best we could, and ended up earning ourselves 1,100 Vietnamese dong, which is about three U.S. dollars. But it was enough to get us to our next stop and through our next task, which was making bricks out of coal. Peter and I fell badly behind because we got lost traveling on the wrong bus to the little village and were the last ones to arrive at the task. But we put our heads down and truly worked as a team, and, by the end managed to climb our way from ninth place to fifth.

All of which begged the question, would we be able to continue working as a team?

※

After a day of crawling through the rice paddies of Hanoi, I was dying for a good night's sleep; this being *The Amazing Race,* that wasn't likely to happen. Our crash pad that night was an upgrade from the hostel/prison, but frankly, staying at the Ramada Inn in hell would've been an upgrade. Our hotel was a fleabag, with piles of dirt on the floor, and tangles of hair in the bed . . . but at least it was air-conditioned, so it wasn't a total loss. I mean, as far as I know, hell doesn't have AC.

But my adrenaline kicked in when I found out what that day's task was: Climb a cliff, a craggy, curved cliff shooting straight out of the Indian Ocean. The Great Wall was nice and smooth, and that was a bitch; this mass of rock was going to be ten times more difficult. I was scared shitless and felt farther away from home than I'd ever been, both literally and figuratively. Aside from my D.N.F. (which is tri-speak for "did not finish") at Ironman, it was the most difficult day of my life.

We were the fourth team to reach the cliff, so I was at an immediate disadvantage. At the Wall, we had a nice little lead, so I was able to sort of take my time; now, I'd be forced to haul ass, and climbing a cliff with one good leg and one busted prosthetic wasn't conducive to hauling ass.

For the first and only time on the *Race,* I was flat-out scared. The climb on the Great Wall was on land, and this was on water, which should have comforted me because falling into the water was far more appealing than splatting on concrete. But this climb was a lot higher. *A lot* higher.

Using only my arms, I inched up the rope, sweating, grunting, talking to myself, silently cursing—remember, the microphones were on, and I wasn't keen on the thought of my grandmother hearing me swear on prime-time television—desperately trying to keep my footing with my one-legged leverage. Getting to the top was indeed harder than the Wall, but I made it, and my success was as much mental as it was physical. You see, I broke it down into time increments: *You can do this, Sarah, it'll be okay, you only have to climb for five more minutes . . . only four minutes, four minutes of your life, and you never have to climb a cliff again . . . three*

minutes, that's a commercial break . . . two . . . one . . . done.
Mind over matter. Brain over cliff.

Rappelling to the ground on the other side of the cliff felt unbelievably sweet, almost on the level of finishing a triathlon. I came in fifth place, which, taking everything into consideration, wasn't that bad.

❈

Our tasks were wildly diverse, and moving from country to country was always a logistical nightmare, but in some ways, the *Race* became a single massive challenge: Wrangling crocodiles at the Madras Crocodile Bank in Chennai, climbing a tower in Kuwait, solving a puzzle in Arabic, it all blurred together. Our challenges were different, but somehow, all the same.

The toughest constant was the continued deterioration of my team's emotional and mental state. Peter's attitude remained snippy, and his unshakable belief in his rightness was infuriating—as was his crush on Dustin Konzelman, the blonder half of Team Barbie. I didn't particularly care that he was trying to make time with her—God knows *I* wasn't going to date him—but his inability to focus on *us* rather than *himself* was becoming a problem.

It all came to a head in Kuwait.

Our task seemed simple enough: Make our way to a place called the Kuwait Camel Racing Club. (More camels. Yikes.) But as was the case in Mongolia, the road signs and maps were about as far from the English language as you could get, and Peter and I were triathletes, not linguists. Reading Arabic was an insurmountable problem.

We stopped at a trio of four-star hotels and asked for directions, assuming that a fancy-schmancy concierge would know the lay of the land. Nope. None of them had even heard of the place, most likely because there wasn't an Arabic name for it.

After wandering the streets in search of somebody who looked like they were familiar with the area *and* who spoke English, we ran into an Aussie gentleman who claimed he knew where the Club was: "Oh, yeah, right, I used to go there all the time," he said, pointing over my shoulder. "It's right up that road about a mile, then make a left and keep going for a bit, and it's there on the left side." I rolled my eyes; that was where we'd just come from. We did the best we could to backtrack, but the more we drove, the more lost we got. At sunset, after eight hours of circling, and circling, and circling, with the sun falling like a rock, I lost all hope, and I couldn't stop the tears. I was so proud of our *Amazing Race* so far, and now we were losing because of bad directions and a poorly marked map. Peter rudely told me to stop crying. Nice guy.

I wanted to stay hopeful, and when I saw a friendly face in the parking lot we'd pulled into to regroup, I thought, *Wait, maybe we're near the right place.* We weren't. It was one of the hired guys from Control Risks, the security company used by the race. It was nice to see a familiar face, but this wasn't a good sign. The fact that they'd sent out the military to look after us told me we were in some serious trouble.

And then, our cameraman's cellphone rang. It was Bertram van Munster, producer of *The Amazing Race*. The cameraman gave me the cell. "Hey, Sarah."

"Hey, Bertram."

"You guys all right?"

"Um, I think we're a little lost."

"A little?"

"No. A lot."

"Okay, you know what? You're almost there. Keep going. You're doing great. Don't give up."

I'm not a giver-upper, but the *Race* was turning me into one. "Right. Whatever you say."

The fact is, Bertram had no idea where we were. For that matter, *nobody* on the production team had any idea where we were. I'm sure they figured that since Kuwait's a small place, they'd track us down eventually.

With the night at its blackest and the streets at their emptiest, we stopped again to ask a local gentleman for directions. He pointed to his car, a beat-up red 1974 Cadillac, and said: "I know where you need to go. Come with me. I'll take you there." So we went with him. We really had little choice.

Ten minutes later, we found ourselves at a dark plaza; the only light in the area was coming from the security guard's little hutch. We parked the car, and our new friend motioned us over to talk with the guard. The two Kuwaiti men went back and forth for a minute, then Mr. Cadillac told us we were probably at the wrong place . . . and that somebody had been executed on these grounds an hour ago.

Freaked out, I asked him, "Why are you telling us this?!"

He said, "He thought you two were the camera crew that was sent to cover it."

And then our Control Risks protector appeared out of nowhere. "Get in your car," he growled at me and Peter. "Now. Keep driving. This ain't the Camel Club."

Exasperated, I said, "Can't you just show us where it is? The joke's over. This is getting ridiculous."

He firmly shook his head. "No can do. But don't worry. You're almost there."

I turned to Peter and said, "Screw this. I'm starving. Let's go to dinner. There's a Ruby Tuesday's back at the Kuwait Tower. We're probably eliminated anyhow, so we may as well spend all our money."

Our Control Risks man sighed and said, "Okay. Get in the car. I can't let the production team stand around at home base while you guys are eating at Ruby Fucking Tuesday's. Let's go. Follow me."

That was the moment I knew with one hundred percent certainty it was over. I knew we'd never *been* close to the Camel Club, and we'd never *be* close to the Camel Club. I stared out the window, but didn't absorb any of what I saw. I didn't need to—it didn't matter anymore whether or not I knew where I was going.

✳

At my exit interview for the *Amazing Race* cameras, one of the questions I was asked was whether or not Peter and I would try to give our relationship a go. I almost didn't want to answer, because Peter had become such a nonfactor to me, but this was television, and I'd been taught to play the game. But it broke my heart that my final words to the prime-time viewers of America weren't about how if you put your mind to something, and work hard, and believe with all your heart, you can succeed, regardless of the obstacles, but rather whether or not I'd keep dating a guy like Peter. But CBS wanted to give the world its fluff, which I can respect and be okay with, especially since not too long before *The Amazing Race,* I'd given the world something that I thought was pretty special and magical.

CHAPTER 8

UNFINISHED BUSINESS

I was bone tired after my D.N.F. at Ironman 2004, and even though I wanted to crawl into a bathtub and then a bed for about six years, I hobbled over to the finish line so I could pay respect to the warriors who'd made it through the race. I sat in a chair, surrounded by my entire crew, listening to the announcer, Mike Reilly, proclaim all the finishers an "Ironman," and crying silent, almost peaceful tears. Truth be told, I wasn't as much heartbroken as I was jealous. I was supposed to be one of them. I was supposed to be an Ironman. All the training, all the hours of work I put into preparing for this race, and it wasn't supposed to end like this.

As I took in the racers' joyous smiles, and watched them fall into the arms of their loved ones, I told Mom, "I'm still going to do this. I'm trying again. And I'm not waiting. I'm going to be back here next year." I knew it could be done. I knew I could do it.

Mom said, "You don't have to. It's okay. We all love you, no matter what."

As we walked back to our condo I said, "I can't go out like this. I didn't come this far to not finish—I want to be an Ironman. I trained my butt off for years. I'm not letting it go to waste." I'd already built up a physical foundation, and I didn't want to wait two, or three, or five years, because who knew what would happen in my day-to-day life? What if I got stuck in a job where my bosses didn't care whether or not I finished Ironman? What if I fell in love, had babies, and moved to France? Logistically speaking, I knew that I could handle the thirty-hour-a-week training regimen *now*, but *later* wasn't guaranteed.

The next morning, when a *USA Today* reporter stuck his Dictaphone in my face and asked me my thoughts on the whole thing, I told him, "I have unfinished business here in Kona. I'm going to come back. I'm going to come back stronger." From that moment on, "Unfinished Business" became not just my motto, but my rallying cry. If I wasn't at work, I was working out, and all my free time was dedicated to taking care of this unfinished business of mine. I posted inspirational notes in my car to keep me motivated. I hung up pictures from my failed Ironman attempt on my fridge to remind me of the disappointment, to keep my drive going on the tough days.

Somebody at Cannondale read the *USA Today* article, and within weeks, they started working on a custom bicycle for yours truly. There aren't many tri-bikes built for small people like me, so their designers wanted to come up with something that fit me perfectly. They invited me to the factory, and said, "We'll measure you from top to bottom, and we'll put together a custom frame and everything. We'll do anything you need to help get you to that finish line."

Heading to Cannondale's nerve center in Pennsylvania, I kept thinking, *What with all the special treatment I'm getting here, this is what Lance Armstrong must feel like every single day.* When I arrived at the factory, I was greeted with a big banner that read CANNONDALE WELCOMES SARAH REINERTSEN . . . UNFINISHED BUSINESS, KONA 2005, and it was signed by the entire staff, and everybody in the building was wearing a t-shirt that said "Unfinished Business." I was overwhelmed with the outpouring of love from every level of the Cannondale team. I couldn't wait to see what they came up with.

Back at home, I worked out constantly, and if I wasn't working out, I was working at Ossur, to the tune of fifty hours a week, and even more if I had to travel to a conference or trade show. All the travel was another big hurdle in my Ironman training; I could run more or less any place, but biking and swimming were other issues entirely.

In terms of cycling, the primary annoyance was making sure I had a bike with me in each city, and this meant taking my cycle onto the plane, or shipping it UPS so it would be waiting for me at the hotel. But that wasn't always enough, because many cities in the country aren't bike friendly, or don't have good bike-riding weather in the winter. Blowing off riding wasn't an option, however, so I got a CompuTrainer, a brilliant piece of computer hardware that works like a regular bike trainer; the cool part is that it connects to your laptop, and the software then increases and decreases the tension on the trainer to simulate the hills of an actual bike course. There were dozens of courses in the program, including Kona, so even in a hotel room in Washington, D.C., I could be riding in Hawaii. Unfortunately, there wasn't such a thing as Compu Swim, so I always tried to stay in hotels that had pools. If the hotel had no pool at all, then I would search on the Internet to find swim classes or local gyms that had a lap pool I could use for a day fee. I'd venture to say that I was just about the most intrepid Ironman-in-training in the world.

The whole thing was ridiculously expensive, and a logistical pain in the ass, but I was so insanely focused that I didn't care. I Visa'ed and MasterCarded my way through my training; whatever it cost, whatever it took, it was going to happen. There were so many variables that could happen on the Kona course—horrible winds, flat tires, illness, etc.—that I had to make sure anything I *could* control was *under* control. If the winds were stronger, *I'd* be stronger. If the temperature was hotter, *I'd* be hotter. I wanted to be prepared for anything. It takes years for a triathlete to reach their peak—that's why so many of the top racers are in their mid-to-late thirties—and I'd only been at it for two years, so I had a lot of catching up to do. If I didn't finish the race, at least I'd know that I'd done everything under the sun to make it happen.

※

To get to Ironman again, of course I had to qualify again, and I chose to do a qualifier race in Kona, in order to get more experience on the roads of Hawaii. Peter Harsch also decided to do the race, so we traveled to the Kohala coast together—and remember, this was before *The Amazing Race,* when I still considered him a cool dude. The race went off without a hitch, and I secured a slot for the 2005 Ironman World Championships. On our flight back to California, I told Peter, "I'm going to Kona to do a training weekend later this summer. I want to ride the full bike course."

He said, "That's a great idea. I'm in."

Over Labor Day weekend, eight weeks before the big race day, Peter and I flew back to Kona for our own little training session, and I was hyped. I knew that the best way for me to prepare for Ironman was to actually ride and run on the course, and swim in the Pacific. I wanted to feel the heat and humidity, to ride in the trade winds, and to learn the rolling hills of the Queen K Highway, to know each wave of the ocean.

Peter and I trained our asses off. Mornings meant swims off the Kona pier, and afternoons meant long bike rides or long runs; in between, we refueled with good meals and long showers. We trained—no, we TRAINED—and our bodies and minds were humming at peak efficiency.

My primary goal for the weekend was to crush the full 112-mile bike ride, which I finished in 8:30, and that included several stops to refill our water bottles. It was an awesome, vindicating session, and if I duplicated that on race day, I'd make it to the run, which meant I'd make it to the finish line.

It was a very important moment in my triathlon life. But more important, that's the day I met Dan Evans.

A fair-skinned, buzz-cutted, super-lean Aussie cutie, Dan and I ran into each other at a Kona bicycle repair shop where Dan worked called Bike Works. Dan, who was also on the island getting ready for Ironman, had taken the job at the shop to subsidize his training. He recognized me right away, because, as I found out later, he had a video of the previous year's Ironman, and, in preparation for Kona, had watched it twenty-five jillion times. (Sound familiar?) I mentioned to Dan that Peter and I were also prepping for Ironman, and he invited himself along on our training ride. Fair-skinned, buzz-cutted, super-lean Aussie cuties don't come along every day, so I told him he was welcome to join us.

As soon as Peter and I got into the car, Peter said all sing-songy, "He likes you, he likes you."

I said, "No *way!* He totally doesn't! Do you think he does? Some of those other mechanic guys were cute, too." It was all very high school, but I didn't think much of it beyond that moment, because I was only focused on taking care of business.

The next day, we met Dan at the bike shop, then made our way to the Queen K, and launched into our training ride. Dan and Peter zipped ahead of me—Peter always zipped ahead of me when we rode together, and I had no problem with that, because I'd have felt guilty if I'd slowed him down on his training run. When they got a few miles down the road, Dan asked Peter, "Do you think we should wait for Sarah?"

"Nah. She's used to it."

Dan said, "Just because she's used to it doesn't mean it's the right thing to do." So he dropped back, and I caught up with him at the ten-mile mark, and he then stayed with me for the entire ride. Now here's a guy who finished an Ironman in 9:09—to offer perspective, the record, held by Luc Van Lierde, is 8:04—and my projected time was somewhere around the sixteen-hour mark. So not only did Dan cut his speed down by one third just to hang with me, he gave me some excellent riding tips—he knew the course up and down, and he told me about the false flats, and when to do certain shifts, and where the hottest areas were and it was all incredibly helpful—and we chatted, and flirted. He eventually asked me if Peter was my boyfriend, I told him no, and said that Peter had another girlfriend back in California. Along the ride I discovered that we had a ton of common interests beyond triathlons, like he was a music freak—he used to work as a DJ and spin house music at some clubs in Melbourne—he loved to dance, and he was a vegetarian. Plus he had that goofy Aussie sense of humor, and he had me laughing and smiling for most of the 112 miles. It was a great day and a great ride.

The weekend was far from perfect, though. The next day, Peter and I went to Spencer Beach Park, where we were going to do a swim/bicycle ride combo, so we could get one last crack at Hawi, the biggest hill and windiest section of the bike course. Hawi was over fifty miles away from where we were staying . . . which is why it sucked when I realized I'd forgotten to bring my bike shoe. It wasn't like we could turn around, zip back to the condo, and grab the shoe, and it wasn't like I could go on a ride without it. After mentally beating myself up for a couple minutes, I told Peter, "Listen, we'll do the swim together, and then you can go on your ride, and I'll go for a run." I needed the bike training, but if I got in a good run, at least the day wouldn't be a total loss.

The swim was lovely—how could forty-five minutes in the warm Pacific not be?—and my run turned out to be pretty okay, too. When I returned to base camp, there were a whole bunch of messages waiting for me on my voice mail, all from Peter, all along the lines of, "Oh. My. God. The wind is so insane that I can't even stay on my bike. You have to get in the car and come get me. Where are you?"

By the time I started the car to go on my Peter search, he wheeled into the parking lot, looking like, well, like he'd taken a bike ride in a near-tornado. Huffing and puffing, he said, "I'm so glad you ended up not doing the ride, Sarah."

I was glad, too. Peter had once finished Ironman in under ten hours, and if he said the wind was bad, then the wind was *bad*. Had I been out on the road, had I had to turn back before I finished a ride due to the conditions, that could've crushed my spirit.

Nonetheless, I had a meltdown. What with the ever-increasing time I had to put in with my job, and the uncertainty of how I'd perform, and the fear that the winds might be that heinous on race day, the pressure of *living* all caught up to me. Barely able to speak because of my bawling, I told Peter, "I don't know if I can do this. What if I can't do it? I can't do my job while I'm training. I can't. I don't know, maybe I'll have to take a leave of absence. There's so many people watching and I can't let them down. I don't want to disappoint Ossur, or Cannondale, CAF, or Oakley, or any of my other sponsors, or my family, or . . . "

Peter interrupted, "A leave of absence is an awesome idea. I'm sure Ossur will be fine with that. Hell, the amount of international coverage you'll be getting them from this race is worth way more than you being there for a few weeks." He had a point. The tears came to an abrupt halt.

The following Monday, I marched into my boss's office and said, "I need some time off."

She said, "Okay. How much . . . "

"Like a whole month off."

"A whole month?" She looked a bit shocked, and slowly said "Um, why?"

"Because I need to train for Ironman."

"Ah. I think we can make that work. If you find somebody to cover you at the Las Vegas trade show in September, it'll be no problem."

And it was no problem.

In 2004, I'd landed in Kona four days before the race, which didn't allow nearly enough time to get my head and body together for Ironman, so in '05, I made it a point to get there ten days in advance. It was a bit crazy—an extra week on the island meant spending a whole lot more money than I had—but I didn't want to leave anything to chance.

Arriving in Hawaii for Sarah's Ironman, Version 2.0, was a very different experience from the previous year. I can't say the pre-race prep was any easier or less intense, but there was a sense of ease, a comfort about the whole thing that was almost soothing. It was helpful that between last year's Ironman and my training trip, I'd learned the lay of the land. Kona had become more than familiar—it was almost homey, insane winds notwithstanding. I knew the neighborhoods, I knew the secret parking spots, I knew the cute restaurants. And I knew exactly what needed to be done to get into the perfect physical and mental space for the race.

My family and friends rented a bunch of condos in the same complex as the year prior, and, as was the case at Ironman Version 1.0, Mom, Dad, and their respective new spouses got along swimmingly, but this time, there was a sense of sincerity. Nobody seemed to be putting effort into being friendly; the kindness and positivity of the conversation and interaction throughout the week felt natural and organic. Mom and my stepmother went on grocery and clothes shopping jaunts together, and Dad and stepdad hit the hardware store to get material to make a bunch of GO

SARAH signs. It was a big, fun family party, the kind of party I never could've imagined during one of our knock-down, drag-out therapy sessions, circa 1992. To think of how far my parents had come since the violence and anger of my childhood was mind-blowing. I was so pleased I could bring everyone together, and for the first time in over a decade we felt like a real family.

For the entire week, my crew (aka Team Unfinished Business) worked like a well-oiled machine. Mom set up a spreadsheet schedule for the ever-increasing number of television and print interviews, and Tabi was in charge of keeping the media types in line, a vital position because somebody needed to tell the *Nightline* people, and the Fox-TV people, and the NBC people, and the other three media teams following me around that yes, you'll get plenty of time with Sarah, be patient, be cool. Tabi kept everybody at bay, but those cameras were everywhere, which, serendipitously enough, turned out to be a great help when it came to dealing with all the techies who followed me during *The Amazing Race* the following year.

Tabi was sometimes forced into bulldog mode, most notably the day before the race, when the media firestorm came to a head. As is almost always the case in triathlons of any size, shape, or magnitude, the racers have to check in their bicycle the evening before the event. On the Friday check-in, one of the camera crews was right behind me, and another one was right behind them, and so on, and so on. There were seventeen people, all trying to get up in my business, and it was a bit annoying, but I tried to ignore the cameras and prepare my bicycle. Tabi stepped into the scrum, held up her hands, and said: "Whoa, whoa, whoa, whoa, whoa. You guys all have to relax. Let Sarah deal with her bike, then you can all get your shot. No interviews, though. She has a long day tomorrow, and needs to be off her feet as much as possible. Please respect that." So in order to placate all the crews, I had to put my bike on the transition rack a few times so each TV station got a clean shot. Ah, the media. . . .

Aside from the hovering, omnipresent reporters, that second Ironman felt like it could've been my wedding: All my loved ones made special trips to be with me, all the attention was focused on the bride (or, as it so happened, the hopeful Ironman), and everybody was dressed for the occasion, not in a suit, but rather a yellow t-shirt with the phrase "Unfinished Business" emblazoned in bright orange letters on the front, and all of my sponsors' logos on the back.

It was incredibly touching that these people would fly all the way to Hawaii just to wake up at 5:00 in the morning and stand around until possibly midnight just to catch glimpses of me jumping in and out of the water, whizzing by on a bicycle, running down a highway, then (hopefully) crossing the finish line. These people spent hundreds and hundreds of dollars to see me for approximately six minutes of a sixteen-hour day—which, when you think about it, also is very weddinglike, because really, how much time do you actually get to spend with the bride?

Not much time at all. But they didn't care. They loved me, and it was enough for them to put on their t-shirts and wave at me whenever they could. And that was enough for me, too.

※

On race morning, I awoke at 3:30 after a fitful but somehow restful three hours of sleep, and Mom made me the first of my two breakfasts—I brought another breakfast down to the ocean with me, because the race didn't start until 7:00, and an attack of the munchies was a distinct possibility. (I should note that breakfast #2 consisted of a banana and a Ziploc bag filled with my now-traditional Ironman snack, Pringles.)

I told Team Unfinished Business that they didn't need to get up at 4:00 a.m. with me, that it would be fine if they showed up in time for the starting cannon, but they insisted. It was pitch black in the early morning hours, but there was an electric feeling in the air. After a couple rounds of hugs, kisses, and good lucks, Tabi, who was in charge of getting my prosthetics from one place to the next, drove me down to the pier.

We were among the first people there. After I went through the body marking area and got my number—180, as opposed to last year's 187; believe me, I was psyched to have different digits—I breathed in the saltwater-scented air, gazed up into the sky, and enjoyed the breeze tickling my face. It was a warm, comfortable morning, and the sun hadn't yet risen, but I was well aware that when it did, the Hawaiian heat would be in full effect. Even though the launching area was a beehive of activity, there was a sense of peace in the Kona darkness.

So when the NBC crew's camera splashed their light on me, it was a bit jarring. With the lens trained directly on my nose, it all came crashing down on me again: *The world will be watching. Two hours from now, I'll be in that water. Lights, camera, action.* But here's the thing: All the attention didn't faze me. I was in a great place, at once calm, edgy, and amped. Yes, I wanted to get into the water and kick the Pacific's ass, but I also felt it was important to take in the moment, to make it about more than a race. This was a watershed moment in my life, and I was going to live it.

At 6:00, I put on my Oakley Thumps—a super-cool pair of sunglasses outfitted with an MP3 player—made my way to the pier, and listened to my pre-race megamix, highlighted by the Black Eyed Peas' "Let's Get it Started," the Beastie Boys' "Don't Stop," "Such Great Heights" by the Postal Service and, of course, the required Black Sabbath's "Iron Man." My shades were tinted, so I could stare directly at the rising sun and watch the sky come to life. I was surrounded by cameras, and Tabi was by my side, and a number of racers went out of their way to wish me luck; though I was constantly engaged with people, I was in a peaceful Sarahworld, and right at that moment, that's exactly where I wanted, and needed, to be. The closer we got to 7:00, the higher the sun rose, and the more hyper I got. I tried to relax myself with some yogic breathing, but my body wasn't having it. Because. It. Was. Time.

After the pros started their swim at 6:45, I put on my swim cap and goggles, jumped into the water, and just floated on my back. Most of the other racers were treading water and being generally active, but since I couldn't chill on land, I figured I would do it in the ocean. And it worked.

Actually, it worked too well, because when the starting cannon went off, it scared the hell out of me. I thought, *Man, I've got to get rolling here.*

And I rolled.

This year, this swim, there was no thinking involved, just *doing:* Stroke, stroke, breathe left. Stroke, stroke, breathe right. Repeat. I felt awesome, from top to bottom, arms, legs, brain, soul. I didn't look at my watch until I got to the halfway mark, which I hit in just over forty minutes. The year before, my midpoint split was forty-five minutes. Five minutes shaved off. Awesome. But I had to keep it going. I couldn't equal last year; I had to *better* it. *Had* to.

When I turned back to the shore, when I saw the beach and the buildings off in the distance, I felt a surge of electricity. Without checking the time, I knew I was in the midst of my finest competitive swim ever, which made me push myself even harder, because why be good when you can be better? It didn't matter that my arms were burning; there would be plenty of rest for them during my bike ride. I became obsessed with getting out of the water as soon as possible. Stroke, stroke, breathe left. Stroke, stroke, breathe right.

Finally, I hit the beach. As I was making my way onto dry land, a couple of race handlers asked if they could help me up. I said, "No, I'm good, I've got it." This wasn't because I was trying to prove anything, but rather because I could move faster by myself, and I didn't want to be slowed down in the least, because I wanted my time to fully reflect the fact that I smoked that swim, to the tune of 1:26. After I hopped up the stairs to a waiting chair, I dumped some water over my head to rinse off the salt, and then put on my prosthetic leg and ran into the change tent. I slathered on lots of sunscreen, put on some lip balm (I remembered this time!), threw on my Oakley shades, slapped on my bike shoe, took a shot of GU, one of my favorite gooey energy supplements, and then dashed out to mount my custom built Cannondale bike I called "Unfinished Business."

Pedaling out of the transition area on my flaming hot bike, I felt like I was in the Tour de France: The crowds were standing four-deep on the side of the road, and between the fans' homemade signs and the various race sponsors' vibrant signage, there were colorful banners hanging off of seemingly every surface. The high-decibel shouts from the friends, families, and supportive tri-geeks launched me out of the proverbial chute like a flamethrower. I told myself, *Ride like you're Lance Armstrong.*

About a mile into the bike ride portion of the race, I saw

my crew, in a tight group, all clad in their yellow "Unfinished Business" t-shirts, all screaming their heads off, and waving their signs. My heart swelled and I felt my face break into a huge smile. I knew it would get lonely out on the highway, so I made eye contact with my beloved friends and family and soaked in their support, so I'd have it in my back pocket if things got tough on the Queen K.

Once I hit the highway, as I took my physical inventory, it dawned on me that I felt pretty damn good. But here's the weird part: I was *afraid* of feeling good, because I'd be that much more crushed if the winds kicked up at the Hawi hill, or if my stomach acted up, or if I got a cramp. This wasn't coming from a negative space, but rather a cautious one. Shit happens, and I knew it would be a really, really bad idea to get complacent, so I kept pedaling, and started talking aloud to myself: "C'mon, Sarah. Keep pedaling, keep moving! Let's do it." (I wasn't alone in my talking, shouting, or grunting; mumbling encouragement to yourself was a common thing at Ironman.)

There was no way I could possibly slide fully into a bad space, because the other racers emotionally carried me up and down the highway. At least once a mile, one of my fellow Ironman-wannabes yelled out, "You're gonna finish this year, Sarah," or, "Looking good, girl," or, most touchingly, "I did this race after I heard your story, and I'll see you at the finish line!"

Most every cyclist passed me—I was competitive in the water, but it's hard to get a great time on the bike when you're pedaling with one leg—but I kept plugging along, confident that I'd successfully trained on this course, convinced that I could handle it, convinced that I'd get back to the transition in time. There was a comfort level that an Ironman first-timer could never feel. Had I realized that in 2004, I might not have beat myself up so badly after not making the cut.

And then, twentyish miles out, right when I hit the grooviest groove of my Ironman life, the media trucks rolled up. The NBC crew pulled even with me, and the reporter yelled, "How you doing, Sarah?"

I gave him an ear to ear grin, and, without missing a breath, without dropping below eighteen miles per hour, yelled, "AWESOME, DUDE! I'M IN HAWAII, AND I *KNOW* THIS COURSE, AND THE WEATHER'S BEAUTIFUL, AND I'M GOING FASTER THAN I NEED TO BE TO MAKE IT TO HAWI BEFORE THE WINDS KICK IN, AND IT'S AN AMAZING DAY!" I couldn't stop smiling, which I'm certain pleased all the TV crews, because they knew that considering my Ironman history, there was the possibility I'd be cranky and hurting. (Some people might say that cranky and hurting makes for good television, but I think most everybody would agree that smiling and healthy is way better.)

I checked my watch regularly to make sure I was on schedule, but I wasn't overly concerned about my finishing time; my only goal was to qualify for the run. Okay, that wasn't completely true. For the past year, I'd been carrying around a keychain that said "16:05." One of my friends asked, "Was that your room key from a hotel?"

"No," I said, "I did some math, and came up with that number as my Ironman dream time." If I crossed the finish line in sixteen-or-so hours, great, but getting to the finish line was the important thing.

Hitting 16:05 would require me to finish the bike ride in eight-ish hours. That wasn't all that realistic, considering my nine-plus hour time the year before. There was absolutely no way I could cut a full hour off of my time. It couldn't happen. It wouldn't happen.

And I was right. It didn't happen.

What happened was, I cut an hour-and-a-half off of my time. We're talking 7:34, folks, 7:34! And every minute was fun. Climbing Hawi: fun. Munching on the gummi bears I'd put in my special needs bag: fun. Listening to the dude spinning dance records for us racers at the end of his driveway: fun. Laughing and joking with the race volunteers: fun. Kibbitzing with the media guys: fun. Feeling the sweet-smelling breezes against my face—and not scary headwinds, mind you, but rather *breezes*: *tons* of fun. Peeing on the bike so I wouldn't have to stop riding: oddly fun. Flying downhill at thirty-five miles per hour: *ridiculously* fun.

Seeing my friends and family in their yellow t-shirts waiting for me at the transition area: more fun than I'd ever had in my entire life.

I deliriously bounced off the bike, slapped on my running leg, and changed my shorts, astounded that I was heading off on my run while it was still light out, and that I was in no pain whatsoever.

Naturally by the time I hit the pavement for my run, Dan was an official Ironman—he completed the race in just over nine hours—and he was waiting for me on the side of the road. I was thrilled to see him and, being that I was happy with my time, stopped to give him a hug and a kiss. He drew away and yelled in his goofy Aussie accent, "What're you doing?! You're in the middle of a race! Get going, get going, get going!"

I said, "Whatever, dude. I'm having a great time. This is Ironman, and I'm enjoying the hell out of it, and I'm going to *keep* enjoying the hell out of it."

Soon after my aborted kiss with Dan, the sun went down, and it was the most spectacular sunset in the history of the islands: reds, blues, pinks, oranges, and the very same shade of yellow as my crew's t-shirts. And as is almost always the case in Kona at dusk, the air smelled like flowers.

Nightfall came suddenly, which surprised no one, because once the sun sets on Kona, it's *gone*. The fact that there are very few streetlights on the running course didn't help matters. Knowing that it would be tough for us to race in the pitch black, the Ironman organizers provided us with glowstick necklaces. In theory, that's a pretty good idea, but in reality it's a pain in the butt, because if you wear them around your neck, they bounce onto your chest with every stride; it didn't slow me down, but it was annoying. Also, having a glowstick reminded me of being at a Phish concert, and for me, Phish and Ironman don't really mix. (Luckily for me, thanks to the Reinertsen Media Pack, my path was sometimes lit by a camera. Glowstick, schmostick—I had television crews.)

As I approached the home stretch, TV trucks in tow, I got more and more amped, and when you combine insane ampedness with gallons and gallons of Gatorade, you end up with a full bladder. I had no problem peeing on the bike, because the cameras were twenty-some-odd yards away; now, they were right in my face. Desperate, I called out to the media posse, "Okay, guys, you need to drive up ahead, because I need to pop a squat and take care of some unfinished business." Fortunately, they all realized that an above-the-knee amputee taking a leak on the side of the road *doesn't* make for good television, so they sped up, and I emptied my bladder for the final leg.

I finally started getting tired, so I downshifted from running to a walk/jog, which reminded me of training with David Balsley, the King of Don't-Worry-About-How-Fast-But-Rather-How-Long. A scantily clad male racer from Europe was moving at my pace, also doing a walk/jog combo, and we kept leapfrogging one another; he'd run while I'd walk, and then he'd walk while I'd run. The closer we got to the end of the race, the faster he went, because he'd be damned if he was going to be beaten by a one-legged, five-foot girl.

But there was no way that I was going to be beaten by a dude in a banana hammock and a singlet. So I picked up the pace, left Mr. Speedo in the dust, hit an incline, hit a decline, and there it was, a half-mile away, lit by a heap of massive floodlights: the finish chute.

In the months leading up to the race, I told my friends that if I made it, I was going to walk across the finish line so I could savor every second of it, so I could bask in the moment. But I couldn't walk.

I couldn't jog.

I couldn't trot.

All I could do was sprint. It was a moment I had dreamed of for twelve years, and now I was in it, achieving it, and I felt like I was actually floating. The collective screaming, and clapping, and chanting of "Go Sarah, go!" from the spectators was deafening. (Mike Reilly, who's been the race announcer since its inception, later told me, "Sarah, I have never, ever experienced a crowd like that at the finish line of Ironman. It was unbelievable.") So 5:51 after I started my run, those yellow t-shirts became obsolete. My business in Hawaii was done. I thought I'd cry if I finished Ironman—I am Sarah Whinertsen, after all— but even after Mike Reilly yelled over the loudspeaker, "SARAH REINERTSEN, YOU ARE AN IRONMAN," I was too elated and/or dehydrated to shed a single tear.

My final time was 15:05, exactly one hour faster than my dream time, and it kind of freaked me out. There's no way I would have even dared think that I could break sixteen hours, let alone break it by almost an hour.

The first thing I did after I crossed the finish line was

hug my mother, who was going nuts, waving her arms and screaming at the top of her lungs. I pulled out of Mom's embrace, smiled at the crowd who was chanting, "Sa-*ruh!* Sar-*ruh!* Sar-*ruh!*" then said to nobody in particular, "Um, would somebody mind grabbing me a chair? I'd really love to sit down."

My voice was inaudible over the audience's screams, so I just plopped down on the ground, basked, and—dreaming of a massage, a mai tai, and a shower—started doing some mental math.

Let's see, if I'd have done one minute better on the swim, one minute better on the bike, one minute better on the run, and one minute better at each of the transitions, I could've broken fifteen hours. Damn! If only I'd have moved a little bit faster. . . .

❊

Ironman played an immeasurable role in healing my family. I still believe that seeing me finish in 2005 after the devastation of 2004 made Mom and Dad realize that anything can be fixed if you want it to be fixed. They pushed all their differences aside for me. It's possible that the cosmos didn't want me to finish in '04, because had I completed it, I probably would've said, "One is enough, so thanks for coming to Hawaii, everybody," and Mom and Dad might've left the island thinking, *Phew . . . made it through that . . . don't have to see him/her until one of the kids gets married.*

Had the race not existed, we probably would have been a fractured entity forever, but the realization of my triathlete dreams helped make us whole again. For that matter, it helped make *me* whole. Yes, I would always be part animal, part machine, but knowing that I conquered Kona helped meld those two parts into a single, fulfilled, satisfied unit.

Okay, maybe not exactly satisfied; let's say *somewhat* satisfied. Because there are always going to be other races to run, and there's a chance that I won't be *completely* satisfied until I finish them all.

EPILOGUE

May, 1981, Long Island

The Cold Spring Harbor Soccer League wasn't exactly a breeding ground for future World Cup athletes. The chances of anybody making the leap from Stanfordville to Manchester United were slim to none. It was just a league where a bunch of boys and girls from the 'burbs could get together after school and on weekends to run around and kick balls. No biggie.

When I was six, all the other kids in the neighborhood were signing up to play soccer, and I wanted in. Seeing my brother Peter, as well as our best friends and next door neighbors Kristen and John, wear their cool uniforms and head to the field each Saturday fanned my emerging soccer flames. Being that Mom insisted on treating me like every other child, she was happy to get me into the league, and I was stoked.

But there were some people who weren't.

What with my one working leg and my one awkward leg brace, I wasn't the most likely soccer teammate, but I didn't care. After I got my cleats, my shin guards, my little white shorts, and my yellow jersey, I felt like the coolest kid in town. This was the first time I'd played a team sport outside of gym class, and no matter how many legs I had, I was going to run all over the field and kick the hell out of whatever ball came in my direction. I was so hyped about the whole thing that I wore my jersey constantly, whether or not we had a practice or a game. The shirt proved that I was a normal child, and I didn't want anyone to forget it.

The practices were at the Cold Spring Elementary School, a few minutes away from our house. It was a mixed gender league, but there were only two girls on my team: Sheila and me. Even at the first practice, I could tell Sheila was a good soccer player, and I kind of latched onto her, because right off the bat, she was more sympathetic than most of the boys, who didn't care about me one way or the other.

I didn't expect to see much playing time, but I figured if I worked hard at the game both at practice and at home—if I learned how to control the direction of the ball with my hard brace—I'd get my chances. Unfortunately, no matter how hard or how much I worked, I couldn't get the whole aiming thing down, because, well, I was a six-year-old who was the size of a four-year-old, and had a fake foot. Even if I was twenty-one and buff, it still would've been difficult to direct the ball with my antiquated prosthetic. And don't get me started about dribbling.

All of which was why I was only put in the game during the last five or so minutes of a blowout. And of course the coach, a handsome doctor, and father to one of the other players, who we'll call Coach Cold Spring, only let me play defense. I guess he thought he'd be flogged by the other kids' parents if I turned the ball over near the other team's goal.

My favorite part of the game was halftime, when we got our snacks; the only time I felt like I was a member of the team was when we all drank bug juice together. Soccer became a whole lot of sitting alone on the sidelines, watching and hoping, completely without a place.

As the season progressed, not only did my playing time disappear, but Coach Cold Spring made certain that I was less and less involved in our weekly practices. I was allowed to participate in the calisthenics, after which Coach Cold Spring would say, "All right, Sarah, take this ball and go over there." And then he'd point to the school. "And all you guys, go over there." And then he'd point to the field.

So while the rest of the team worked on dribbling and passing exercises, or participated in a full-blown scrimmage, I was one hundred meters away from the field, kicking a ball against the wall of the school, out of sight, out of mind.

The assistant coach—who looked like Santa Claus's ne'er do well brother, and was a hell of a lot more patient than Coach Cold Spring—came by every once in a while to check up on me, or to give me some pointers, or to offer an encouraging word. Other than that, I was completely alone, kicking the ball, and waiting for it to come back, over and over again, for the entire practice.

Every week, I hoped Coach Cold Spring would let me play with my teammates for even a few minutes, or take a crack at dribbling through the cones, and every week, I was disappointed. It got to the point where I'd show up, grab a ball, and head over to the wall without being told. I'd been programmed.

Near the end of the season, Mom was doing some grocery shopping, and while she was wandering down the cereal aisle, somebody tapped her on her shoulder. "Excuse me, are you Sarah's mother?"

"Yes."

"I'm Mrs. Cold Spring, Coach Cold Spring's wife."

Mom's guard went up. "Can I help you?"

"Well, I just wanted to tell you that Sarah's doing a great job, and working really hard, but, well, I was talking about it with my husband, and we were thinking that maybe there's a more, um, *suitable* activity for her other than soccer."

Mom said, "Mrs. Cold Spring, these children are six years old. This isn't the World Cup. Tell your husband to let her play. And who are you to tell me what to do with my child?" And then Mom grabbed her cart and walked away without another word.

That was my last season of soccer. That was my final crack at team sports.

February, 2008, New York City

Nike, my shoe and apparel sponsor of two years, flew me out from California for an autograph signing and discussion session at the Macy's in Herald Square, and they hyped it big-time, most notably with a quarter-page ad in the *New York Times*. They had been handing out postcards all day in front of Macy's announcing my appearance at the Nike store inside. This wasn't a vacation by any means; it was a business trip, filled with high-powered meetings and fancy dinners, quite the far cry from the deli trays of my *U.S. Olympic Gold* days.

The Macy's people situated us up on the second floor, in a huge area devoted solely to Nike women's shoes and clothes, called "Nike on Two." They set up a huge stage with Nike signage everywhere, video screens with footage of my running, and a disconcertingly large picture of me as a backdrop. On the stage were two directors' chairs and a microphone. It was quite the to-do.

The crowd was far larger than anybody expected: *Amazing Race* fans, triathletes and their families, Macy's employees training for their first marathon, friends, friends of friends, and friends of friends of friends. All in all, we're talking seventy-five people.

Even though it was the dead of winter, I sucked it up and wore shorts, because, aside from selling Nike gear, the point of my visit was to help the layperson realize that if somebody like me can just do it, *anybody* can just do it, and if my prosthetic wasn't out there for the world to see, the message would've been diminished.

I gave a little speech, then the local Nike rep interviewed me for a while and opened up the floor for questions, and then we raffled off some Nike gear, as well as three *Sarah-Bears,* my customized teddy bear with an amputated leg. After the raffle, I came down from the stage and walked over to a table, on top of which sat a pile of posters for me to autograph.

Most everybody who was at the event queued up in front of the table. The first gentleman in line was tall, had gray hair, was wearing a dark trench coat, and looked very familiar. Now I give talks all over the country, and run triathlons all over the world, so oftentimes *everybody* looks familiar, so I wasn't particularly taken aback.

He gave me a big smile and said, "Hi, Sarah."

"Hi! How're you doing? Great to see you!" I pretended I knew who he was, because, well, maybe I did.

He said, "You don't remember me, do you?"

I said, "You look familiar."

He nodded, leaned close to me, and said, "I'm the soccer coach."

I gasped. "Coach Cold Spring. Um. Wow." For years, I'd been telling my soccer story at public speaking events, and it was featured on one of my Ironman television packages, so it was *out there.* But I never really considered that Coach Cold Spring would actually ever hear it. Why would he? Only about a million people watch the Ironman telecast, most of whom I suspect are either triathletes, families of triathletes, or random tri-geeks. If I'd have ever thought about it, I wouldn't have pegged Coach Cold Spring as any of the above.

After we shook hands, he pulled an old photograph from his pocket and put it on the table: our soccer team. He said, "I want you to have this. My number and e-mail address are on the back. You probably don't want to talk to me, but just in case." I was blown away. This guy came all the way from the hinterlands of Long Island to New York City—a ninety-minute train ride—just to give me a picture and his contact information. He came all that way to take care of his own unfinished business.

As I stared at the photo, I realized that my soccer experience was the ultimate positive-coming-from-a-negative situation. Essentially, this childhood soccer league was what sparked my entire athletic career. I suppose I've always been trying to make up for the athlete that I was told I couldn't be when I was six, trying to prove that a woman with a disability deserves her race at the Paralympics, trying to demonstrate that a woman with a disability can finish an Ironman, and should be welcomed on the soccer pitch, softball field, or swimming pool. That has become my life's work and for this, I'm grateful to Coach Cold Spring.

I shook his hand again and said, "I should thank you for putting the fire in my belly. It made me a better athlete, and a better person." I stood up, gave him a hug, and stared at his back as he walked away. After a few seconds, I came to my senses and went back to signing posters.

While I was lying in bed that night, I kept thinking about Coach Cold Spring. This trip had to have been unbelievably difficult for him, and I decided that he'd paid his dues. And the fact of the matter was, he didn't know what to do. It was 1981, and you didn't see disabled athletes on television or in magazines, so he didn't know any better. The coach was probably doing the best he could. Maybe he wasn't coming at it from a perspective of, *She's going to slow our team down,* but rather, *I don't want to set her up for failure.*

Now that he'd made this positive, undoubtedly difficult gesture, I wondered if I should keep telling the story. Did he deserve to have complete strangers think badly of him?

I tossed and turned for another couple of hours and eventually concluded that the story wasn't about him, and it wasn't really about me. It's about being able to achieve your goals, to realize your dreams, no matter what anyone else tells you. It's about being the best *you* that you can be. It's about redemption, and hard work, and inner strength. It's about never giving up, never letting other people squash your dreams because of their own ideas of what you can and cannot do.

It's about living a life without limits, the kind of life that I always have tried, and always will try to live.

SARAH REINERTSEN'S RACING CAREER

Year	Event	Location	Notes
1987	NYS Games for the Physically Challenged	Long Island, NY	
1987	Jr. Orange Bowl Games	Miami, FL	
1988	U.S. National Championships for the Disabled	Nashville, TN	
1988	NYS Games for the Physically Challenged	Long Island, NY	
1988	Canadian National Amputee Championships	Calgary, Canada	
1988	Jr. Orange Bowl Games	Miami, FL	
1989	U.S. National Championships for the Disabled	Nashville, TN	
1989	Pan Am Games	Tampa, FL	
1989	Jr. Orange Bowl Games	Miami, FL	
1990	Jr. World Championships	St. Etienne, France	
1990	U.S. National Championships	University of Ohio, OH	
1991	U.S. National Championships	Long Island, NY	
1992	U.S. Paralympic Trials	Atlanta, GA	
1992	Paralympic Games	Barcelona, Spain	
1993	Paralympic Revival	Duderstadt, Germany	
1993	Irish Games for the Physically Challenged	Dublin, Ireland	
1994	U.S. National Championships	University of Maryland, MD	
1995	U.S. National Championships	Boston, MA	
1997	Flex Foot International Challenge Invitational	Chula Vista, CA	
1997	U.S. National Championships	Springfield, MA	
1997	Paralympic Revival	Duderstadt, Germany	
1997	Georgetown Classic 10K	Washington, D.C.	
1997	Hood to Coast Relay	Mt. Hood, OR	
1997	New York City Marathon	New York, NY	* first marathon
1998	Los Angeles Marathon	Los Angeles, CA	

Year	Event	Location	Notes
1998	Rye Derby 5-miler	Rye, NY	
1998	Adidas 7 sisters 12-mile Trail Race	Massachusetts	
1998	Transcontinental Tri 4 Life (Run only)	Chicago to NYC	
1998	San Diego Triathlon Challenge (CAF relay team)	La Jolla, CA	
1998	New York City Marathon	New York, NY	
1999	Los Angeles Marathon	Los Angeles, CA	
1999	U.S. National Championships	Fairfax, VA	
1999	Revlon Womens' 5K	Los Angeles, CA	
1999	Paralympic Revival	Duderstadt, Germany	*Set world record 100m
1999	New York City Marathon	New York, NY	*Part of TV crew on NBC
1999	World Track & Field Championships	Barcelona, Spain	*Set world record 400m
2000	Millennium Marathon	Hamilton, New Zealand	
2000	U.S. Paralympic Trials	Hartford, CT	
2000	Marabana ½ Marathon	Havana, Cuba	
2001	Kona ½ Marathon	Kona, Hawaii	
2001	ASPIRE 10K	Plainview, NY	
2001	Cow Harbor 10K	Northport, NY	
2002	Brooklyn ½ Marathon	Brooklyn, NY	
2002	New York Mini Marathon 10K	New York, NY	
2002	ASPIRE 10K	Plainview, NY	
2002	Freedom Run 5K	New York, NY	
2003	Carlsbad Triathlon	Carlsbad, CA	*first triathlon
2003	San Diego International Triathlon	San Diego, CA	
2003	Pat Griskus Sprint Triathlon	Waterbury, CT	
2003	Holliston Lions Club Triathlon	Holliston, MA	
2003	Camp Pendleton Triathlon	Oceanside, CA	
2003	Solana Beach Triathlon	Solana Beach, CA	
2003	Mission Bay Triathlon	Mission Bay, CA	
2003	Malibu Triathlon	Malibu, CA	

Year	Event	Location	Notes
2003	ITU World Championships	Queenstown, New Zealand	* first triathlon world championships
2004	Boston Marathon	Boston, MA	
2004	Wildflower Triathlon	Lake San Antonio, CA	
2004	Escape from Alcatraz Triathlon	San Francisco, CA	
2004	Buffalo Springs Lake ½ Ironman	Lubbock, TX	*first ½ Ironman
2004	Malibu Triathlon	Malibu, CA	
2004	Ironman World Championships	Kona, HI	*first Ironman attempt
2005	Wildflower Triathlon	Lake San Antonio, CA	
2005	*Runner's World* ½ Marathon	Allentown, PA	
2005	Honu ½ Ironman triathlon	Kona, HI	
2005	Lifetime Fitness Triathlon	Minneapolis, MN	
2005	San Francisco ½ Marathon	San Francisco, CA	
2005	Santa Barbara Triathlon	Santa Barbara, CA	
2005	NYC Triathlon	New York, NY	
2005	Ironman World Championships	Kona, HI	*1st woman on an artificial leg to finish the Hawaii Ironman
2005	San Diego Triathlon Challenge for CAF	La Jolla, CA	
2005	Silver Strand 5K Run	Imperial Beach, CA	
2006	ESPY Award Winner	Los Angeles, CA	Disabled Female Athlete of the Year
2006	*Runner's World* ½ Marathon	Allentown, PA	
2006	Wildflower Triathlon	Lake San Antonio, CA	
2006	*The Amazing Race* (season 10)	USA, China, Mongolia, Vietnam, India, Kuwait	*1st amputee to compete on the hit CBS reality series

Year	Event	Location	Notes
2006	NYC Triathlon	New York, NY	
2006	Osh Kosh Triathlon	Osh Kosh, WI	
2006	Timberman Triathlon	Gilford, NH	
2006	Chicago Triathlon	Chicago, IL	
2006	Malibu Triathlon	Malibu, CA	
2006	Philadelphia 8K Run	Philadelphia, PA	
2006	Dana Point Turkey Trot 10K	Dana Point, CA	
2006	San Diego Triathlon Challenge for CAF	La Jolla, CA	
2007	Wildflower Triathlon	Lake San Antonio, CA	
2007	USA Triathlon National Championship	Hegg Lake, OR	
2007	NYC Triathlon	New York, NY	
2007	Shawnee Mission Triathlon	Kansas City, KS	
2007	Avia Pacific Coast Triathlon	Crystal Cove, CA	
2007	Reykjavik ½ Marathon	Reykjavik, Iceland	
2007	ITU World Championships	Hamburg, Germany	
2007	Nike Women's ½ Marathon	San Francisco, CA	
2007	San Diego Triathlon Challenge for CAF	La Jolla, CA	
2007	Silver Strand ½ Marathon	Coronado, CA	
2008	South Beach Triathlon	Miami, FL	
2008	Wildflower Triathlon	Lake San Antonio, CA	
2008	Fargo ½ Marathon	Fargo, ND	
2008	Accenture Escape from Alcatraz Triathlon	San Francisco, CA	
2008	Buffalo Springs Lake Ironman 70.3	Lubbock, TX	
2008	Accenture Chicago Triathlon	Chicago, IL	
2008	Nike + Human Race 10K	Los Angeles, CA	
2008	Malibu Triathlon	Malibu, CA	
2008	Nike Women's ½ Marathon	San Francisco, CA	
2008	San Diego Triathlon Challenge for CAF	La Jolla, CA	
2008	Muddy Buddy	Los Angeles, CA	

ACKNOWLEDGMENTS

This book wouldn't have been possible without a whole circle of family, friends, and supporters. I am grateful to Michele Martin and Steve Harris for giving life to this project. Alan Goldsher, my partner in this book, who helped me find the right words for all my life moments. Thank you for all your patience, guidance, and good cooking! Tim Mantoani, thanks for a great cover photo. To Lara Asher and the whole gang at Globe Pequot Press for believing in me and holding my hand through the process.

To Ossur, for giving me the prosthetic technology that allows me to run, walk, leap, and bound, in a life without limits. Especially to Tabi King who helped launch my triathlon dreams. Joni Schneider for being my Ossur mom, Oddny Bjornsdottir and Eythor Bender for their unwavering support, and to Jon Sigurdsson and Edda Geirsdottir, who cheered for me from Iceland.

To the Challenged Athletes Foundation, who believed in my Ironman dreams from the start. A special thanks to Virginia Tinley, Bob Babbitt, Jeffrey Essakow, and the office staff Lauren, Jill, Barbi, Jennifer, and Marie.

To my friends at Nike—you inspired me as a little girl to "Just Do It" and run even before I dreamed of making sports history. I am proud to wear the Swoosh, and I am particularly grateful to the guys in the Kitchen who have given me sole, Mike Friton and Tobie Hatfield. Christie Farin, for believing in me, Lauren Westendorf, Lori Roth, and the whole gang at Olympic Sports, Nike Women, and Nike Running for taking such good care of me.

The Cannondale crew, including the staff at the Bedford factory, you make the best bikes in the world. Thanks for the sweet ride. I am incredibly grateful to Bill Rudell, who has been the hub of all my bike support since my first Ironman attempt.

A Step Ahead Prosthetics, and Erik Schaffer, who have made me the finest prosthetic legs for more than a decade, because of you I have a collection of legs that not only make me fast, they make me feel beautiful.

To the fine folks at Oakley, especially Greg Welch who has supported my triathlon endeavors since I first landed in California. Thanks for the rockin' Oakley sunglasses, and for hosting that fabulous "Amazing Race" party.

Cytomax has been my drink of choice for years; I'm thankful to the entire family at Cytosport, especially Nikki Brown for all the fuel to keep me going in training and on the racecourse.

To my friends at USC and Swim with Mike, especially Mara, Ron, and Mike—you changed my future, and I'm proud to be part of the Trojan family—Fight On!

To my coaches, mentors, and training partners, without your support I never would have gone the distance. Paddy Rossbach was the spark that ignited the fire; you have been my mentor in sports and in life. You made me ASPIRE higher. David Balsley who taught me to run and live "a little bit crazy," and his wife, Maggie Nimkin, who always supported our adventures. To Paul Huddle and Roch Frey for turning me into a true Ironman. Mickie Shapiro, Lee Gould, Larry Davidson, Phil Kreuter, Mike Collins, and Peter Harsch for supporting me along the way. To Hank Iglesias at EDGE Cyclesport, thanks for keeping my bike tuned and my wheels spinning.

To the Ironman *ohana*, Ben Fertic, Diana Bertsch, Mike Reilly, Blair LaHaye, and Peter Henning. A big *mahalo* for all that you have done.

To the many race directors who have hosted me at their events, Terry Davis and the gang at Tri-California, Rick Kozlowski, John Korff, Dave McGillvary, Keith Jordan, Mike and Marti Greer, and Michael Epstein. Especially to Mike and Sue Polanski and the whole Greater Long Island Running Club.

To Jill Krementz, for documenting my story and above all for introducing me to a life long friend, Eli Wolff. My fellow Sarah, aka Sarah Rosenberg, you told my story to the world better than anyone, because you lived part of it with me. To the Williamsburg Track Club, Lisa, Caroline, Dale, Adam, Howie, and team chef, Lara. My other track sisters from the U.S. and World Games, Lindsay Nielsen and Jami Goldman-Marseilles.

Wendy Ingraham, thanks for taking me under your "Wing." To Holly Bennett for all the GU a girl could ever eat. Eric Gilsenan for hooking a sister up. And to all the other people and companies who helped me, Profile Design, Zipp Wheels, CompuTrainer, Giro Helmets, *Triathlete* Magazine, *Competitor* Magazine, B&L Bikes, and Think ASG.

To my friends at *Runner's World* magazine, especially to the Chief Runner, Bart Yasso; you have encouraged me for many years and I am grateful to you and Laura for your friendship. Thanks for all the miles and smiles. Speaking of miles, many thanks to CBS and World Race productions for the adventure of a lifetime.

Brian Lorenz, for bringing life to the SarahBear and helping me launch my Always Tri brand, you have been a friend and a true visionary. I am indebted to you forever.

Karen Demasi, my New York mom, and IMG boss, you made me a TV star and producer. Thanks for being a colleague and a dear friend. Jerry Leeds, who discovered and encouraged my talent as a speaker during those early days on Long Island. Thank you for mentorship and support. To Susan Gordon Ryan, for all those track meets and memories, thank you. To my extended family at King of Kings Lutheran Church and Camp Koinonia, thank you for taking care of me all those years. You each hold a special place in my heart.

Heather Prendergast, for being my best friend since driver's ed class, thanks for always listening. To the Iron Crew, Chris and Sue Lockwood, Kristen and Jonathon Croxton, Claire and Denny Richman, Sandy and Brett Prior, thanks for coming to Kona and cheering me on.

To my parents, thank you for your years of love, care, and belief. I am grateful to have such a wonderful brother, Peter. Thanks for putting up with such a tough big sister. To Pedro and Joan, who have gone above and beyond and made me feel like their daughter. To *bestemor*, Dorothy and Simone, and *bestefar*, Iver, for teaching me to be a strong Viking woman.

My best friend and love, Brooke Raasch, you are a constant source of joy in my life. I feel lucky to have found a man of strength and integrity. Thank you for your enduring love and support.

ABOUT THE AUTHORS

Sarah Reinertsen is a motivational speaker, addressing corporate audiences across the country. As a world-class athlete, she competes in dozens of races every year. Sarah also leads a series of sports clinics and mentors other athletes, with and without disabilities. She lives and trains in Orange County, California. This is her first book. To find out more, please visit Sarah's official Web site at: www.AlwaysTri.com.

Alan Goldsher is the author of seven books including *Hard Bop Academy: The Sidemen of Art Blakey and the Jazz Messengers* and *Jam: A Novel*. As a ghostwriter, he has collaborated with numerous celebrities and public figures. For more information, please visit Alan at: www.AlanGoldsher.com.